50 Y
for J

Evelyn Booth-Clibborn

New Wine Press

New Wine Press
P.O. Box 17
Chichester PO20 6RY
England

ISBN 0 947852 57 3

Unless otherwise stated, Bible quotations are taken from the Authorised Version. Bible quotations marked NIV are from the Holy Bible, New International Version. Copyright© 1973, 1978 International Bible Society. Published by Hodder & Stoughton.

Typeset in Plantin by The Ikthos Studios, Jolly's Farm, Chute Forest, Andover, Hampshire.
Printed and bound in Great Britain by
Richard Clay Ltd, Bungay, Suffolk

Contents

Acknowledgements

My deep gratitude to Angela Butler for her advice and encouragement in helping me to arrange the material for this book; and also to Sylvia Alexander for her willingness and generosity in typing the manuscript.

Foreword

I was delighted when my dear Aunt Evelyn asked me to write a few words of introduction to this book which tells the story of God at work in her long and varied life. What is written here is certain to be an inspiration to many. For me, reading it has brought back some vivid memories of times when our paths have crossed. When I was at school in North Devon, I cycled down on several occasions to see my grandmother, the Maréchale, at the Haven, the house on the edge of Dartmoor so vividly described here.

I remember receiving then a warm welcome from Evelyn and from that wonderful and saintly woman Adèle, whose devoted service helped the whole Booth-Clibborn family to survive tempestuous times. It was on that very tennis court where Evelyn was given the words of her first chorus, as described in Chapter 16, that I walked with my grandmother, and she told me to "Go for the highest, Stanley". Undoubtedly her words played a part in my decision to enter the ministry.

Evelyn devoted those years to caring for her mother to the end of that full and remarkable life. As this book shows, she has helped very many people to find a living faith in Christ.

It is in His service that her great musical gifts were always used. I remember to this day our house in North London echoing to the strains of a Chopin Scherzo as she rehearsed it with great skill on the piano in our lounge.

She has never married, and yet like St. Paul she has had many children in Christ. She has been richly blessed in her friends and like others who will read this memoir, I am deeply grateful to Angela Butler for her help in bringing out in book form these personal memories of "E. B-C". She has fought a good fight in her long life, and the record here will be a blessing to many.

October 1989

Stanley Booth-Clibborn
Bishop of Manchester

Prologue

"Stand up and bless the Lord,
Ye people of His choice,
Stand up and bless the Lord your God
With heart and soul and voice."[1]

These are the words that lifted my heart in praise and thanksgiving, as I completed this book.

For some time I had felt a growing constraint to put together a written record of how God has blessed my life and work. All I know is that I simply had to write it as a more permanent affirmation of His hand upon my ministry.

Since the most positive awareness at my 90th Birthday gathering was that of 50 years of dedicated service to God — the result of a total commitment I made to Him in 1938 — I felt I should give some idea of the 40 years which preceded it.

From what I heard her say, I think my Mother felt very deprived when Catherine Booth (her Mother) decided against her receiving a higher education. No doubt this was why she was determined that I should have the opportunity to develop my talent for music.

Every morning before breakfast during my school-days came that all-important hour at the piano. After years of concentrated and

1. James Montgomery (1771-1854). Hymns of Faith, no. 3.

uninterrupted practice, I secured two music diplomas L.T.C.L. and L.R.A.M.

In 1922, Mother took me with her to America, where she placed me in a highly recommended Bible School in New York. Though the teaching there was deep and thorough, I cannot remember any outstanding spiritual experience.

Not long after this an opening came to teach music in a large Quaker School. I rejected this because of the restrictions it implied. At that time, I was far more concerned with maintaining my liberty than in seeking the mind of the Lord.

Earnings from private coaching in music and French proved slow and inadequate, and finally I had to take a job as a filing clerk in a large bank on Wall Street.

Any touch of the Spirit there may have been upon my life seemed, as I entered this cold, strange world, at its lowest ebb. The cause of my misery lay far deeper than the endless rows of tall, steel cabinets.

All the while, my family and friends were praying for me. On my very first day, as I worked among the filing cabinets feeling totally lost, a wonderful wave of God's love swept over me, as though assuring me that, if I had forsaken Him, He had not forsaken me.

"Stand up, and bless the Lord,
The Lord your God adore;
Stand up, and bless His glorious name
Henceforth for evermore."[2].

Although my arthritis means that I now need more care, I am not retiring from active service.

One who found the Lord as her Saviour at a

2. Ibid.

Recital-Talk I gave in June this year wrote afterwards, "I have always believed in Christian principles, but never thought that Jesus could be so real."

"Thanks be to God who gives us the victory through our Lord Jesus Christ." (1 Corinthians 15:57).

October 1989

Chapter 1

Recollections from Childhood

"They loved not their lives to the death,
Christ only — their soul's vital breath."[1]

I was born into a large family of five boys and five girls. Our parents were utterly devoted to the cause of Christ. My father, who came from a distinguished Quaker family, gave all his linguistic and literary talents to the spread of Christianity during the pioneer days of the Salvation Army. My Mother, eldest daughter of its founder, General William Booth, and widely known as the Maréchale, founded that movement in France, and later, with my father, in Switzerland.

Our parents' calling meant that they were away from home a great deal, and we were entrusted to the care of able nannies, governesses and tutors. During our earliest years we lived in Europe, where the Salvation Army was rapidly extending its activities. For a time, our home was in Holland, where I was born, then in Belgium, and later still in France, after which most of us finished our education in England.

French was our first language. It expressed the earliest and most intimate experiences of our

1. To Sing Thy Praise, Book 1. Evelyn Booth-Clibborn.

childhood. We younger ones learned German under governesses. English came quite naturally as it was spoken by our parents and we finally settled in England.

There were many attractions during those early years: the cat, with its periodical family of kittens; the tortoise escaping, to be found walking sedately down the street; the croquet on the lawn, with its wild excitement of sending balls "to Jericho". Most thrilling of all, while living at Westcliff-on-Sea, were the trips down to the front. With everything piled into Father's bathchair, (previously used by him during a time of disablement), we would dash all the way down the steep incline to a dazzling, sparkling sea.

But it was our Christmases that were the highlight; pure, glittering magic. The tall tree would be lit from top to bottom with glowing candles, one of my brothers standing guard with a wet sponge on top of a broomstick. We celebrated in the Continental way, on Christmas Eve, with the gifts laid out to view along the base of the tree. We children recited poems or Bible passages we had memorised, and sang carols in English, French and German. Then, before handing out presents, Mother and Father would give us a brief talk on spiritual matters.

We both felt and admired deeply our parents' self-sacrifice and love for Christ and the souls of men. I can see now the radiance on my Mother's face as she spoke with passionate intensity of lives reclaimed from sin, darkness and despair. Then would follow my Father's own moving testimony to the grace and saving power of his Lord, with perhaps a verse or two from his well-loved hymns.

Oh, the glow of these occasions!

While both my parents were actually proving the deeper truths of our faith, it was perhaps my Father's special contribution to us as a family, and indeed to thousands besides, to have expressed them in such fine and memorable hymns. One is still frequently quoted:

"There is no gain but by a loss.
We cannot save but by the cross.
The corn of wheat to multiply
Must fall into the ground and die.
Oh, should a soul alone remain
When it a hundred-fold can gain?

Wherever you ripe fields behold
Waving to God their sheaves of gold,
Be sure some corn of wheat has died,
Some saintly soul has been crucified.
Someone has suffered, wept and prayed
And fought Hell's legions undismayed."[2]

We were very carefully guarded by those who were in charge of us children. Even so, the frequent moves from country to country, with their inevitable separations, left their mark upon our young lives.

Never can I forget the intense grief at having to leave France whilst still a child. My younger sister and I were brought to England by our French Governess. This auburn-haired young woman would sing a haunting melody which I recall to this day. It symbolised all that we were leaving, and I was heart-broken. How unbearably attractive she seemed compared with the two staid

2. Arthur Sydney Booth-Clibborn

aunts in whose care we were left in this utterly strange country. I am sure these relatives were very kind and excellent people, but my childish heart, frightened and desolate, took refuge again and again in that sad little refrain — all I had left of my beloved France.

I had an older sister whom I greatly admired. She had both poise and charm, and how easy it had been to weave an aura of enchantment about her. But the day came when she accompanied my Mother to America. I stood on a piece of land jutting out into the sea, and watched the great steamer that was bearing her away until it was out of sight. I can even recall the song the orchestra was playing, as it was gently borne across the waters. It was a soft spring-like day, but my heart was as bleak as a deserted beach in mid-winter.

Such partings were very distressing. My parents felt them keenly, especially in earlier years when my older brothers and sisters were very young. I can remember Mother relating how, one evening, during a campaign in Le Havre, news came from Paris that one of her little boys, aged two years, was dangerously ill.

After a great inner conflict and committing of the matter to God, she decided to stay at least one more night. "I shut my feelings up in a room in my heart," she told us later. "Now you can cry all you want, I told my heart; I am going on with the meeting." And go on she did, speaking with great power, followed by such blessing. The very next morning came a reassuring telegram.

It is an illusion to imagine true Christian dedication does not imply sacrifice. Even when we regard the discipline of sacrifice as a privilege, it must touch every part of life, including the closest of ties. And as a family we did not escape.

Chapter 2

The Discipline of Music

"Heavenly Father,
Gracious Father,
Here to Thee we raise
For Thy kindness,
Pardon, goodness,
Deepest praise."[1]

I remember the touch of revival upon our home before we left Westcliff-on-Sea. It was a visitation of some depth, and I was acutely conscious of the waves of intense prayer and exaltation all around me. "Evelyn is always weeping over her sins," commented one of my parents somewhat uneasily. I suppose I was such a highly-strung child. But there is no doubt that I received blessing, although this experience did not prove to be very deep or enduring.

In view of my drift in later years, the opinion was expressed that I could not have been a child of God at all then. I cannot be positive about this. All I know is that, in spite of the indefiniteness of the period, I had always spoken to God as His child, and sincerely desired to please Him. That was a long way from the total abdication of my will.

1. To Sing Thy Praise, Book 2. Evelyn Booth-Clibborn

The tragedy is that if the pleasing of God is not the desire and purpose of the whole being — a matter of entire dedication — the intrusion of other lesser interests is inevitable, with the result that the supreme objective loses force and eventually ceases altogether.

The pull of the lesser good, the purely secular, is so compelling that only a heart wholly fixed upon God can hope to triumph and sing the song of victory. Many years were to pass before words came to me which expressed this certainty:

"Thanks be to God,
Thanks be to God,
Who giveth us the victory
Through Jesus Christ our Saviour,
Thanks be to God,
To God."[2]

Not long after my sister's departure with Mother to America, we moved to London, a step that marked a notable change in the character of our lives. Several members of the family had gone, or were going abroad; studies were intensifying and the daily routine had become more exacting.

A cold bath would start each day; then for my part I would be down in the basement dining-room practising the piano before breakfast. After this would come school and homework. Constant attention would be given by our governesses to the correct speaking of German, and always, like hurdles for a competing horse, the next examination loomed into sight.

Because I was so highly strung, these tests,

2. To Sing Thy Praise, Book 2. Evelyn Booth-Clibborn

although usually passed with honours, were a minor form of torture; so also were the public performances. I recall early on, while nervously playing one of Mendelssohn's "Songs Without Words" at a students' concert, my legs jerked up and down to such an extent that I was in absolute terror lest this should be noticed by the audience.

Something of my sorry state must have been conveyed to the Head of our Academy, for, when everyone had left, he gently asked me to repeat my performance. Such special attention by so important a person was balm indeed to my shattered confidence.

Whether I suffered or not, concerts and examinations had to go on, until, with great relief, I had gained my second and final diploma. Yet not without one special failure, all the more devastating for being the only one I had ever known in music. That particular examination, a very advanced one, was, I believe, stiffer then than later. I was still going to school when the minor catastrophe occurred. Having been called into my Mother's room, I promised, amidst many tears, that I would attempt it again. Perhaps it should be mentioned here that, owing to extreme tension, never in all my examinations could I do reasonable justice to my musical ability.

Shortly before that second attempt, my teacher, in her anxiety for my success, took me to play the required selections before the sister of one of the greatest authorities in pianoforte playing, who literally tore my work to pieces. I was utterly crushed, and it was a profoundly dejected pupil who returned with her teacher to North London that day. But I passed the examination when it came.

All this concentrated study of the musical classics developed some fine perceptions and sensibilities, but it failed signally in drawing me any nearer to God. It would seem that the good, however worthy or beautiful, can easily distract us from the best.

One spiritual experience, nevertheless, does stand out. I had obtained my two musical diplomas and I found myself on the eve of a new departure.

I attended the Keswick Convention with one of my sisters. It was perhaps the richest experience I had ever known until then. Together with a group of Christian students we tramped up hill and down dale in that glorious countryside. As we went, we sang the hymns we had learned in the tent meetings. The impression of the messages and hymns was woven into the very texture of those days, and the depth and sweetness of two of those hymns, as felt then, has never been wholly lost.

This is the chorus of one of them:

"Living, He loved me; dying, he saved me;
Buried, He carried my sins far away;
Rising, He justified freely for ever;
One day He's coming — O glorious days!"[3]

And here are a few lines of the other:

"Loved with everlasting love,
Led by grace that love to know,
Spirit breathing from above,
Thou hast taught me it so."[4]

It was to be a long time before I would know again such a fresh and spontaneous spiritual experience.

3. J. Wilbur Chapman (1859-1918) Hymns of Faith, no. 133.

4. George Wade Robinson (1838-1877) Hymns of Faith, no. 334.

Chapter 3

The Pull of America

"O long hast Thou waited
While I have resisted,
My pride had but kept us apart."[1]

It is not easy to approach the second period of my life, with its radical changes, both inward and outward, so deeply at variance with the best I had been taught. There was much that was good humanly speaking, but also much that must have grieved the Lord, making easy the drift away from what was His perfect will for my life.

I sailed with Mother in the early twenties, into what seemed a totally new world, the United States of America. It was a great wrench to leave England and I made wild promises about being back soon; but many years were to pass before I finally returned to stay.

Of the voyage over I remember little, and it was not long after my arrival in America that I entered a Bible College highly commended by other members of the family. I had spent one brief term at a similar college in England, and no doubt Mother hoped that after this further instruction I would be prepared to assist her in her work. It was easy for me to fall in line with

1. To Sing Thy Praise, Book 2. Evelyn Booth-Clibborn

these arrangements as I had as yet no clear idea about the future.

The time at Bible College was not without its impact, but I do not think that even then I had come to grips with the basic implications of true discipleship. Over-familiarity with spiritual things can breed assumptions which have no actual foundations. Only a complete committal of heart and mind to Christ, as I have since learned, with a reliance on Him alone, can enable us to walk His way in the world.

I had begun to visit a friend of the family who ran a very successful hotel in the Westchester County of New York State. This lady, an Australian, went out of her way to make me welcome among her guests. As occasions arose, she encouraged me to play the piano for their entertainment.

I did not visit many places of entertainment, but the lightheartedness of young America, so very new to me, was heady wine indeed. It was all so easy, so charming, so subtly distracting, this floating along on the surface of life, with people who did not seem troubled by any deeper issues. It appeared harmless enough at the time, even a kind of relief from natural tension; nevertheless, it prepared the way for a worldly attitude of mind wholly foreign to the sacrificial calling of a true Christian.

Some time later my Mother asked me to cross over to Ireland to help her in her evangelistic missions there; when I arrived, my uncertainty of mind and lack of purpose in spiritual matters became only too apparent. I felt that I could not agree to become part of her work and at the same time remain true to myself, as I saw it then, and true to her, as well as to the work. The strength of her personality was then at its height, and I believed that it might destroy such self-expression as I might have gained, and that seemed so desperately important to me then.

It later turned out that my decision not to continue with her was not without remedy so far as my Mother was concerned; others of her gifted children came to her aid. But in view of all the musical training she had provided for me, and the help my playing would have been in her work, it must have been difficult indeed for her to understand. For us both, it was a sad time; but my choice was made and I yearned to get back to America.

My fear that this desire might be thwarted resulted in a nightmare. I was on a ship returning, as I wished, and the waves so buffeted and impeded its progress, that I awoke in a state of panic. It was a time of intense inner turbulence; a mind and heart in unrecognised revolt.

As I look back, although there had been considerable truth in my reasoning, for I both despised hypocrisy, and had not the slightest craving for the limelight so incessantly focused on my family, I now see that the cause of my action lay far deeper.

Somehow, somewhere, the spirit of rebellion had taken root; that same spirit, in however modified a form, that hurled Lucifer from the heights of heaven into the abyss of hell. I believe it was from that moment that my path took a definite course away from God's direct plan for my life.

Oh, the folly of thinking we can ever know what

is best, once we are cut off from the source of divine wisdom! What desolation must then inevitably catch up with a life that has once known the touch of God.

Chapter 4

Life in New York City

"O love of God that seeks us still,
Broods over hearts grown hard and chill."[1]

My return to America brought me face to face with an entirely new situation. During my absence, the Australian lady, who had made me so welcome before, had married my Uncle Herbert, musician of the Booth family. Whereas previously I had seemed to matter in some small way, her world now naturally revolved around her husband. It was understandable that Uncle should wish me to seek a position elsewhere to earn a living; but with my uncertainty of mind, and lack of practical experience, it was to be no easy task.

Events came to a head when I realised he had found an opening for me, as a music teacher, in a well-known Quaker School. I had become increasingly unhappy with the change of circumstances, but, no doubt because of the years of discipline under governesses, the idea of entering any kind of institution simply appalled me. My decision was swift and bold. Under no circumstances would I live or teach in a school. The consequences of that earlier decision made in Ireland to return to America at all costs had caught up with me.

My Uncle's personality was a forceful one,

1. To Sing Thy Praise, Book 1. Evelyn Booth-Clibborn.

although not as dynamic as my Mother's, and I knew I might not be able to stand up to him. I, therefore, made the desperate resolve to prepare to leave, but only to tell him I was going on the eve of departure. It was a most painful interview for both of us. I could appreciate that he had done what he thought was best for me, and I had determined to say nothing I would ever regret. In this, I believe I did not fail, but it was the only comfort left to me following that sad episode.

I moved to the poorer part of the town, where I started teaching music with a hired piano, and giving lessons in French conversation. I had little money and progress was slow.

Meanwhile, news of my movements had reached the family, and one of my sisters came in real distress to see me. I also had a stinging letter from another relative accusing me of having too high an opinion of myself and of being over-ambitious. This, actually, was not true. I lacked altogether the confidence so essential to advancement, and ambition was only to come much later, and then only for a brief time.

Though my sister viewed my humble surroundings with deepest distress, I at least had the satisfaction of feeling myself to be free at last. Yet how dearly was I to pay for that hard-won liberty! How long before I was to discover that true freedom, far from resting on personal independence, lay in the most complete dependence on Christ alone.

To supplement my small earnings, I tried to obtain additional work as a musician, but I lacked the necessary recommendation, as English diplomas were not recognised in the States. Through the influence of an acquaintance, I was able to secure a position as a filing clerk in one of New York's largest banks. After one or two moves, I decided to share with friends I had met at my Aunt's hotel, which they had left owing to financial difficulties. These charming and cultured people, mother and daughter, had from the first shown a very kind interest in my welfare. I soon discovered that they were penniless, and from that time on, for many years, I supported all three of us with my earnings at the bank.

I have always been thankful that I was prevented from living what might have been a wholly selfish existence at that particular time. There was the joy of sharing, and of talking things over with two people who were alert to the finer points of life and never-failing in their sympathy and interest.

Just after we moved to New York City (to avoid my long commutings backwards and forwards to the Bank), Mother, with her secretary, again visited America, and once more pleaded with me to help her in her missions. By now, I was caught up with my new way of life, and still lurking was the fear of having to leave America.

But perhaps the most significant of all was the pain and the sense of guilt, far more marked this time, at having to refuse Mother's request. It hurts even now to think of that lunch we had together in the Pennsylvania Hotel.

At the bank, I had to make tremendous adjustments. No words can describe how lost and fearful I felt in the strange world where I now found myself. Though the tall steel cabinets of the filing department hid nothing more sinister than hundreds of banking files, they presented an awesome challenge. Even when given the simplest work, I seemed almost paralysed through fear. Needless to say, my feeble fumblings were not lost to those in charge.

I suppose I must have been something of a mystery to the smart, fast-moving citizens of a great metropolis. Matters did not improve when I refused to be drawn into the usual intrigue and gossip of the department; nor did it help when it was discovered I could both play and act.

On one occasion I took the leading part of a Cockney girl in the bank's annual play, following which the President came in person to congratulate me. Well do I remember the morning after a shrill young voice called to me over the tops of the cabinets, "Don't forget you're only a clerk in the filing department!"

They were difficult days but the balance was maintained by my obvious inadequacy in the work. Did the Head of Department perceive, I wonder, the inner sense of failure and insecurity I sought so desperately to hide? One day, when deeply embarrassed over being found out in yet another fault, I exclaimed, "Miss Jones, why don't you fire me?"

"Fire you?" came her prompt reply. "What on earth would happen to you?"

My slowness in seeing a joke, highly amusing to those quick-witted Americans, also helped to make my position a little easier. This was specially so when I would join in the general laughter on account of some interpretation of my own — probably quite false — of a joke that had been made. Inwardly, I was only too relieved at being an accepted part of the group if only for a moment.

It was, in fact, a revolutionary re-adjustment to

a completely new way of life. God no doubt permitted this lesson in discipline because I had feared the constraints of his higher way. Yet at the same time I revelled in being one of a crowd, hidden behind the walls of a large office building in a great city. One of my brothers, a gifted speaker and writer, would say to me on the occasions we met:

"Why be a little fish in a big pond? Why not come out West with me and be a big fish in a little pond?"

But that is what he could never understand. The last thing I wanted was to be a big fish in a little pond. The swing away from public life was complete. Yet to some of the family, my attitude must have remained a complete mystery.

The predominant characteristic of my fellow-workers, as it seemed to me then, was a rather brittle superficiality. This would often be reflected in the empty, almost cynical laughter; and yet, the kindness I had already seen in Miss Jones was also to be found in others. Looking back, I can remember the helpfulness of one whose remarks had been the most caustic of all. Perhaps the most startling fact was that I was given a rise in position and salary; and Miss Jones, for reasons best known to herself, eventually sought my opinion about various ones in the department. It was a great joy that she felt she could trust my judgement.

Yet those last few years at the bank brought an increasing sense of heaviness and futility. I recollect vividly the moment when, as I was sitting at my desk near the large swinging doors, a sudden conviction flashed into my consciousness: "This is only a passing phase. My life is moving to some other destiny."

Chapter 5

My Concert Début

"Oh restless soul, dost thou not see
God's great provision made for thee?
Dost thou not hear His gentle voice
That bids thee, weary one, rejoice,
And wait in calm expectancy
For grace in thine emergency?"[1]

When, around 1930, the great depression hit New York, my services at the bank being more or less dispensable, I found myself without a job. I was given a generous bonus, but this was fast draining away. My two friends and I were then sharing a flat in up-town New York City. Fortunately, the daughter had started to earn, so we somehow pulled together and were just able to keep things going.

Suddenly, and most unexpectedly, the door to the musical world opened. A Christian musician, through the influence of a mutual friend, became interested in my talent. He had been a pupil of Letchitiski, teacher of Paderewski, the world-renowned pianist, and was himself a teacher of some note. When he heard me play, he offered to give me lessons free of charge, and prophesied that in four years' time I would be making my

1. To Sing Thy Praise, Book 1. Evelyn Booth-Clibborn.

début as a concert artist. This literally came true.

I was now back in a very familiar world, but a far more exciting one than in the past. It was the finest teaching and the most advanced form of piano-playing I had ever known, and I was able to put them to frequent test at my professor's fortnightly recitals for his pupils.

For the first time in my life, I was seized with ambition. I desired intensely to make the grade, and no effort was too great to perfect my art. I spent as much time at the piano as my strength allowed. Although six to eight hours' practice is average for a concert pianist, I was never able to do more than four hours a day. But the whole tempo of my life increased enormously, and there was always new work to prepare for the next performance.

I had also started to compose music, and was much encouraged by authoratitive opinion to continue along this line. Eventually, I rented a large studio in the Steinway Building, Carnegie Street, containing two grand pianos, where I taught and gave pupils' recitals, filling the room to capacity.

It was actual playing that still held the centre of my attention. I was reaching a new level of performance. It was thrilling yet exhausting. One outstanding experience was when I played before a capacity audience in the exquisite red and gilt Aeolian Hall on Fifth Avenue before a famous French critic. Can I ever forget playing from memory that twenty-three page Bach Fugue?

Events seemed to be moving rapidly, when there came a serious set-back. My professor decided that he would present to the public first a pianist who was my senior by many years. She was, in fact, technically more advanced than I was and certainly more confident on the concert platform. I was to pay dearly for this decision. The effort of sponsoring her recital in the Town Hall completely drained our teacher's resources. I well recall the moment, after a lesson in his studio, when he told me he could not now finance my début.

It was a crushing blow. I had stood aside for this other pianist, working at fever pitch for the time when it would be my turn — and now this! As I stood there, a flood of emotion swept over me, and I wept. Then, suddenly, I knew it could not be, it must not be, and, in that instant, hope lit up the whole of my dark sky. It lay in just one word, "Mother"!

Such is the twisted path of our sheep-like wanderings, that, in my extremity, I was to turn to the very one whom I had twice so deeply disappointed, when she, in her need, had turned to me. But nothing could now stop the course of events. My professor stood with me at the entrance of the Subway that night, and I was embarrassed to see the shame and misery he could not hide because he had let me down. But the thought of Mother, like a draught of fresh sea air, was fast rallying my powers together.

Dear, valiant Mother! Twice, in very turbulent periods of my life, she helped as no-one else could have helped: now, in a course which was the outcome of my own will and way; and later, when God directly intervened in my life. Mother's response to my plea was prompt, and I was soon sure of her financial support. My zeal knew no bounds. My teacher, too, was borne along on the stream of a new hope. The Town Hall was booked and we launched into extensive preparations.

A time of great strain began. Quite apart from the high standard of performance required, there was the expense involved, which still largely depended on my own efforts. Coming just when, musically and physically, I needed to be in top form, all this exacted a toll of time and energy, which I could ill afford. Was the way already being prepared for what was to come?

I knew that if I could find sufficient buyers for the Town Hall Boxes, and at high enough prices, this would raise more money than all of the individual seats together. Débuts are notoriously difficult to finance. Mrs. Johnson, a Christian friend of considerable means, who had already helped me professionally, bought the two centre boxes. Mrs Ballington-Booth, who helped her husband, my Uncle Ballington, to found a religious movement, The Volunteers of America, also bought a box. Very soon, practically all the boxes were sold.

Meanwhile, we were busy over individual tickets. It was here that Miss Jones, my supervisor in the filing department, came to my help. She sold tickets throughout the Bank. She had kept in touch with me, and it was she who had brought me my first music pupil.

Shortly before the recital, I was taken to the basement of the Steinway Building to select a piano for the occasion. From one end of the large room to the other were Steinway grands which had been used by distinguished artists, each one an exquisite instrument and in perfect condition.

It was not an easy choice. The selected piano having been installed on the Town Hall platform, I played my programme through to my professor alone. He seemed pleased with my performance, yet, for my part, its very smoothness made me uneasy for the début the next day.

I do not want to give unnecessary details of the performance itself, or to dramatise an event which occurs frequently in the musical world. Yet, because it is part of my story and because of all that happened later, I do want to give a fair account of this unique experience in my life.

The recital took place in the evening, and the Hall was nearly full. I was extremely nervous. Though accustomed to a certain tension in concert work, this was, to say the least, a very special test.

As always with a début, the critics would be present. Every note and innuendo would be judged. My future as a concert artist hung in the balance. Moreover, this was taking place in a city which could command the greatest names in music. The standard was of the highest.

I had no illusions about my work. My technique, I was told, was not equal to my gift of musicianship; and I lacked the toughness so essential to the demands of the concert platform. Yet here I was, about to face a most knowledgeable and critical audience. It seemed like venturing forth into a terrifying world, one that could easily crush all the combined hopes and efforts of years. Thus I reached one of the most crucial moments of my life. That evening, as I mounted the platform at the Town Hall, and walked towards the piano, in front of a considerable audience, no one was further from my thoughts than God.

My performance, though by no means one of my best because of general nervousness, drew many hopeful signs. After my first number, "Twenty Variations on a Theme by Corelli" by Rachmaninoff, my professor rushed backstage to say that it was a good beginning, and that the impression was very favourable.

The critics stayed on for the second half of the programme, which was considered a good sign; and the reception given to my own pianistic composition, "Ballade Quasi Sonata", was in the nature of an ovation.

The press comments on the following day varied; some were very encouraging. One of the works I played was Chopin's B flat Sonata, but strangely enough it was my rendering of his Funeral March that made the greatest impression. The Times, New York's most important newspaper, spoke of my "sound musicianship", and the Herald Tribune wrote favourably of my composition, hinting at the possibility of another recital.

It was a big step forward, even though I was only on the lower rung of the ladder of success. During the months that followed, I became increasingly aware of an underlying dissatisfaction and restlessness. The preceeding year had been one of great strain; therefore, some form of reaction was probably inevitable; but this seemed to go much deeper.

My prospects were good. I had just been asked to link up with an Italian School of Music in the Steinway Building; and I had been offered, as a pupil, the most brilliant performer I had taught. Why, then, did a haunting sense of failure and of utter futility persist?

I cannot say when the truth dawned on me, but, very gradually, the conviction was borne in upon me that this acute inner depression was linked to my failure towards God. The distance which now separated me from the Lord, the estrangement that existed between us, showed how far I had drifted.

Chapter 6

Crisis

"You walked among men, Lord, You know the way;
You bore the heat and the toil of the day;
You walked alone, Lord, to Calvary's tree,
There You were crucified, Saviour for me."[1]

Can the light ever be wholly lost once it has penetrated the soul? I have proved that, even if not lost, its eclipse can be total. The accumulation of unspiritual thoughts and actions can become so great that a chill of darkness descends upon the soul. Strange, in that darkness, how dim are the outlines of our achievements.

Whatever our reasonings at the time, that gradual forsaking of the Christ-mind and the Christ-way, that dulling of our spiritual sensibilities, through sheer neglect, is not a joyful process. Neither are the steps back, once there has been a turning to God, and the journey has begun towards that place, perhaps far distant, where we left off.

The Kingdom of God, which Christ said should be the primary objective, had been so completely overshadowed by the Kingdom of this world, in relation to security, personal interests and art, that

1. To Sing Thy Praise, Book 1. Evelyn Booth-Clibborn.

it was inevitable my contact with God should recede, and finally disappear. That which had been my spiritual life, however weak, was now an arid wilderness.

Twice during the earth-bound preoccupations of those years, the light shone through. The first time was not long after I had begun to drift away from God; and the second was shortly before my return to God. In neither instance was the light exprcssed in some message or vision. There is no other way of describing it except as an overpowering sense of glory, which, like a radiant warmth, penetrated and enveloped my whole being.

The key-note on both occasions was joy, an indescribable joy, unlike anything on earth. Why should I have been given these two experiences? A musical career might not be wrong for another Christian; but, for me, I know that I personally was right outside God's will. I speak strictly for myself.

Yet, however far away, I was still a child of God. Could those two experiences have been a tender reminder that, though I had forsaken Him, He had not forsaken me? And that, whatever my coldness and my indifference, His love and His faithfulness remained unchanged?

Such moments of special visitation are very rare. God's laws, though tempered with mercy, are inflexible. My life, with its multiple causes and effects, had to take its course; and, apart from the grace of God, there were no short cuts. Now, indeed, I began to reap what I had sown. The separation of my life from the only true good, the years of purely secular interest, bore their fruit of darkness. How could I come through this dark valley, this midnight of the soul?

My position was solitary indeed. I was approaching a major inner crisis, yet I could not breathe a word of it to anyone. My many friends were worldly, religion meaning little or nothing to them. It was the same with those who were closer to my personal life, the dear friends with whom I lived and had shared so many interests in the past. I think that their seeming casualness was prompted by a lurking fear that, with my religious background, I might one day re-enter Christian work.

Just as remote was the possibility of discussing my problem with anyone in my own family. Most of them were thousands of miles away, and had taken for granted my absorption with secular interests. Though I had occasionally attended services at various churches, I had never joined any place of worship or taken part in its activities. So, in every way, I was cut off.

Thus it was that, without the help of my friends, relatives, or church, I came to the great turning-point of my life. Indeed I doubt whether any of these human agencies would have availed, so completely had I cut my moorings.

Morning after morning, in my room at the further end of our flat, I woke to silent tears. There seemed so little meaning now to all that I had struggled to build up. Like a house disappearing over the edge of a crumbling cliff, the self-erected building of years was vanishing from my sight, and with it went the confidence I had so dearly bought.

Some part of that building had been good; at least, my musical career had been creative, and stimulating to others as well as to myself. But what of its foundations? Certainly God had no part in it.

Clear as the light are Christ's own words: *"And everyone that heareth these sayings of mine, and doeth them not, shall be likened unto a foolish man which built his house upon the sand".* (Matt. 7:26).

Aand did not God say through the apostle Paul: *"Other foundation can no man lay than that is laid, which is Jesus Christ"?* (1 Cor. 3:1).

For the Christian, whatever his gifts or aptitudes, this is the only true test of a life and of work.

In the darkness and loneliness of my spirit, I sought God, but could not find Him. I stretched out my hand, as it were, but there came no answering pressure. I prayed, but there was no response; my very words seemed empty and meaningless. I felt lost in a vacuum of total isolation, groping for a contract which had ceased to be. At last, weary with such striving, I challenged God, "Your words says that, if we seek You with all our heart, we will surely find You. Please give a word."

One morning very early, before the din of traffic had shattered the silence of dawn, I got up from my bed, and under a strong compulsion, went to a corner of the room where there was a small table; on it was a large Bible.

Lifting the old volume and carrying it to the bed, I lay with it resting on my body. It was as if its weight were a part of that greater burden which was bearing me down. With a silent prayer, I opened it, and my eyes fell on a passage I had never as yet seen or heard:

"Remember not the former things, neither consider

the things of old. Behold, I will do a new thing; now it shall spring forth; shall ye not know it? I will even make a way in the wilderness, and rivers in the desert." (Isaiah 43:18-19)

I stared at the words. Again and again, almost incredulously, I read them. Those ancient lines were coming alive there in my room, centuries after they had been written; and they fitted my situation as a key fits a lock. Had God uttered them audibly, they could not have been plainer or more timely.

Light was breaking through the thick darkness of my spirit, and with it, even though dimly, the dawn of a new hope. God was speaking to me through the written word, and I was listening as never before, with an intensity born of my extremity.

"Remember not the former things, neither consider the things of old." That was just what I had been doing — remembering, regretting, repenting. But repentance itself, however deep and essential, could not bring deliverance. I was still in the dark.

"Behold, I . . ." God was turning my eyes from my own utter helplessness to Himself, the only one who could meet my need. *"I will do a new thing . . ."* So He had a definite plan. The wonder of it was beginning to grip me. *"Now it shall spring forth . . ."* How my new-born hopes seized upon that word *"now"!* *"I will make a way in the wilderness, and rivers in the desert."* I was only too well aware of that bleak, inner wilderness; but there was to be a *"way"* and *"rivers"*.

Then, spreading warmth where there had been nothing but a blinding cold, came the realisation that God still wanted me. He, the One I had by-passed, ignored, dishonoured, was still wanting me.

A *"way"*, *"rivers"*, still I pondered those words. It was the pursuing of my own way that had brought me to this crisis. There could be no rivers until I was on God's way. The order is very clear: first the way, and then the rivers.

No word of condemnation of my independent spirit and distant wanderings was spoken. In spite of my shameful neglect, he was placing His infinite grace at my disposal. It was this indescribable, incomprehensible love of God, that brought my already penititent heart straight into His hands. At the same time, came the knowledge that, through Christ my Saviour, my sins were forgiven, blotted out for ever.

I have tried to put into words something of what happened at that most sacred moment. This, in substance, was my prayer of committal to God: "If, dear Lord, You still want me, if You can yet do a new thing with my life, and even now lead me through this bleak wilderness to the rivers You have promised, then I now yield my heart and life into Your hands, never, never to withdraw them again."

In the silence of that little room, without the sound of voice or instrument, without vision or sense of exaltation, that quiet act of dedication was made, which affected the whole course of my life.

Whatever the trials, temptations or failures in the years that have followed, I have never again sought, or even desired, to take back my life.

Chapter 7

Turning Point

"Crushed with a sense of my failure and loss,
All seemed to me but in vain;
Then light broke through in a glorious tide,
Gone was my darkness and pain."[1]

The turning point had been reached. I had "come to myself" in the strict privacy of that little room in New York City. Like the Prodigal, I had seen my condition as one of utter hopelessness apart from God. There are striking words in Isaiah chapter fifty-three:

"All we like sheep have gone astray, we have turned everyone to his own way; and the Lord hath laid on Him the inquity of us all". (Isaiah 53:6).

This seems to show that such independence from God which had been my undoing is the basic and universal sin. It requires the atoning death of Christ to make a reconcilliation between us and God. I had arisen and returned to my Father who had hastened to meet me. This brought me inevitably to the Cross of Christ my Saviour where my sins were cleansed for ever, making possible a renewed fellowship with a holy God.

1. To Sing Thy Praise, Book 1. Evelyn Booth-Clibborn.

I was still a long way off from my inheritance, as was the Prodigal. God had yet to bring me all the way back to where I forsook His way; but at least now I was conscious of His presence with me, and what a difference that made!

My relationship with God had been put right. He began by restoring me at what was the weakest point, my health. I was considerably run-down. Quite unexpectedly, Mrs. Johnson, who had already so generously supported my début, offered to place me under a special course of treatment. This was at her own expense, and in a comparatively short time I was restored to complete health and strength. God knew that this was essential for what was to follow.

During this period of recovery, it became clear that I would need to hold myself in readiness for any new development in God's plan. The thought that I might have to leave my dear friends of many years' standing was deeply painful. I remember walking up and down Broadway in the greatest distress, wondering how I could ever bring myself to take so hurtful a step. But, as I prayed, this was more and more impressed upon me.

Two incidents stand out in that time of deep depression. One day in our flat, when my friends were out, I was suddenly arrested by a remark from our lodger, an elderly and very cultured New England lady, who was standing by the sink as I passed through the kitchen. She was a very reserved person, and almost a stranger, which made her comment all the more startling: "This is not the right place for you".

Her words were brief, and not unkind to anyone,

but they revealed an assessment of my position that astounded me. Aware of my loyalty to my friends, I could make no reply, except to thank her for her interest; but the relief of another's understanding, even if only partial, was indescribable. Her words seemed a verbal confirmation of my most hidden conviction.

Another day, when I was again alone in the flat, except for our lodger who was in her room, I had wandered into the sitting room, depressed over the step to be taken, and all the failure that had led to it. As so often, I sat down at the piano. Suddenly, without warning, I was singing and playing entirely new words and music. They seemed to come by direct inspiration from God and with great force:

"All power have I", "All power have I",
"All power have I in heaven and earth",
For great is our God, and great is His love,
And great is the fulness that comes from above.
"All power have I", "All power have I",
"All power have I in heaven and earth" [2]

The impact was dynamic. It was as if God were telling me not to keep on going around and around the little pond of my life, with its failure and regret. I was to look beyond it to the vast ocean of His love and its height, its depth, and its length. He seemed to be saying: "Come out and lose yourself in Me, in my limitless power and all-sufficiency".

Later I put verses to that chorus to give some idea of the circumstances in which it was written;

2. To Sing thy Praise, Book 1. Evelyn Booth-Clibborn.

here is one of them:

Self is a prison confining the soul,
Blotting out light with its wall.
Self is but death, it is God who is life;
He is the answer to all.
"All power have I" . . .[3]

So tremendous was the joy and exhilaration which now seized me that I had to run to our staid New England lodger, and pour out with all my soul this fresh revelation. I have never known to this day her reaction to it all. Perhaps it is just as well. Certainly, I gave her something to think about. Might not this also be part of God's plan? Eventually, the leading was clear that I should tell my friends of my decision to leave; but I shall not dwell on that time.

What sorrow we bring to others as well as ourselves, through being out of God's will. He was creating externally, as well as inwardly, His own way through my wilderness. My outer life had but taken its form from my inner spirit of independence from God. Let me say again, however, that a musical career in itself is not wrong. God does not always lead us out of situations. Our path is to obey at whatever cost. This, I have discovered, is the only secret of continued inner peace and wisdom.

I had been able to rent a furnished room, large enough to hold my grand piano and other necessary furniture. As I moved into my small quarters, I experienced an extraordinary sense of release. This confirmed to me the deep conviction which had led to this step.

3. To Sing Thy Praise, Book 1. Evelyn Booth-Clibborn.

Not long after, a letter came from my Mother asking me if I would accompany her on a tour of Australia. My mind at this time was occupied with the further building of my musical career, and I felt that the suggestion was out of the question.

Then swiftly came the thought: "Mother is doing God's work, and you are now in His control. Suppose it were His will for you to go? Suppose it were His will for you to give up your career altogether?"

At that moment, Africa came before me. As a young girl, I had always been afraid that God might send me to Africa. It was, indeed, the old rebellion against the idea of becoming a missionary, which came rushing back. This inner conflict brought a veil of darkness over my spirit which lasted two or three days.

Suddenly, I could stand it no longer: "Yes, Lord," I said, "Africa it shall be if You wish it, Australia with Mother, or anywhere else You may want to send me." The veil then lifted, and, in this connection, has never returned.

As it turned out, God did not send me to Africa, or even to Australia. Mother had made other arrangements during my hesitation. But the battle had been won, and, according to God's wisdom, prepared me for what lay ahead.

It was not long after this experience that I saw unmistakably that it was God's will for me to return to England. Because of the recent inner victory, I could view the letting go of all I had built up with a serene mind; not so my colleagues, friends and relatives. Had I carefully considered? Was I sure? To some of them it must have seemed sheer madness to let go of a career just as it was becoming stabilized.

Yet the urge persisted: "I must leave for England, and the boat I must sail on leaves on February 8th." It was now early 1939, on the eve of world-shaking events. I had no idea of this. One thing alone was certain. The command was His; the obedience must be mine.

How was I going to get the money for the fare across? Here indeed was a problem. No immediate money was available. Then I knew. I was to approach Mrs. Johnson who had already been so kind. She was the only one among my friends who could advance me such a loan.

Yet how could I do this? Had she not already been extraordinarily generous? Had I not prided myself on the fact that I had never asked her for a loan? What would she think of this sudden decision on my part? My reluctance at having to approach her on such a matter was quite indescribable. But God's hand was upon me, urging me on.

A luncheon date was arranged, and I shall never forget the shame and the misery I felt, as I paced up and down in the Museum of Arts on Fifth Avenue, trying to pluck up courage to go to her house.

As soon as the meal was over, Mrs. Johnson led me up to her spacious library. When we were seated, she immediately turned to me, "What is the matter, Evelyn? I can see you are troubled about something. Won't you tell me what it is?"

Haltingly came the words: "I feel God wants me to leave for England, and that He wants me to sail on a ship leaving on February 8th. Would you . . . could you . . . possibly make me a loan of the fare, to be paid back after I get home?"

"But, of course. How much do you want?" came the quiet, matter-of-fact reply. I stated the amount. She had risen from her seat, and was now at her desk. "Yes, but you will want more than that," she added, still matter-of-factly, and briskly filled in the cheque.

How faithless I was. And how much God still had to teach me. Needless to say, the entire sum was paid back within three months of my return. Loans may not always be the best way, but this experience had been part of the road back; an unforgettable lesson in humility and obedience.

How can I describe the journey back to England? I had a deep conviction of the rightness of everything, and an extraordinary sense of freedom. As I paced the decks, the surging inner joy was at one with the drive of the wind and the waves. I had a long, long way to go on the road to dicipleship, but, at least, I was on the way. And the Lord was with me.

Chapter 8

The Return

"Peace, peace, God-given peace,
Deep in my soul doth abide;
Though pain and care I must know,
Jesus is near at my side."[1]

When I landed at Southampton, a little red beret sitting jauntily on the side of my head, I was full of happy anticipation and thrilled beyond words. But the welcome from my relatives was rather sombre. What, oh what, was this cloud threatening my radiant sky?

Then my brother spoke: "Father is dying. He fell down the steps to the back garden, and it affected his heart. He has been asking for you."

"Father . . . dying?" I echoed, as in a dream. I was trying to grasp this totally unexpected development. "When did this accident happen?"

"On February 8th."

February 8th. I remembered that driving urge: "I must leave on the ship sailing on February 8th"

Once I read somewhere: "God is never a moment too soon or a moment too late."

If a sombre note was sounded at my arrival,

1. To Sing Thy Praise, Book 1. Evelyn Booth-Clibborn.

there was none at the departure of this man of God, this warrior of many battles in the cause of Christ. As we stood round his bed, singing some of his hymns, my Father was radiant. Could it be joy over the return of the prodigal, so long prayed for?

"His poetic gift, which in the hands of God inspired him to write some great, immortal hymns, never left him alone. Night and day, ceaselessly, his songs would rise and flow. It seemed as though his soul could never express enough the glory, the wonder, the all-sufficiency of his God."

I quote the above from some words of mine included in my Mother's booklet, "A Poet of Praise. A Tribute to Arthur Sydney Booth-Clibborn".

It was significant that at the start of my consecrated life God should wish me to have the privilege of witnessing the glorious climax of another dedicated life, one that had been faithful from the very start. It seemed an unmistakable seal on my return, as if my Heavenly Father's warm hand had been placed in benediction upon my new life.

The realisation that God was bringing me back to the very place from which I had strayed, at the side of the Maréchale, my mother, was to come later. Meanwhile, there was even further confirmation of my rightness in coming home.

My first night back in England was spent in a small room on the first floor of our old home in London. I had never liked this Queen Anne House, tall, dark and narrow, with its memories of governess-controlled days and unceasing examinations. Yet here I was, at the end of many far-distant wanderings, having left my musical career, my friends, and America itself, back in this tiny room of the old house, the future a complete blank. Now, indeed, if ever, I would know for certain whether God had brought me here or whether it was a tragic mistake.

I woke very early the following morning. It was very dark and very still. As is often the case in times of extreme change, I was instantly aware of the complete difference in my surroundings. But before my thoughts could take form, an ineffable sense of peace invaded my whole being.

I have often tried to describe the quality of that peace, but without success. Compared to it, I had never yet known the meaning of the word. Can it be that we do not often go far enough in our obedience to make such discoveries possible?

As I lay there in the dark — body, soul, and spirit submerged by that wave of unutterable peace — a new song was born in my heart out of the intense realisation of that moment. It is not a song in the accepted sense, neither is it a hymn. It is a reaffirming of my entire dedication to God. I have often sung it when relating the experience, for it is of the very essence of that early morning.

"Thrice won, I come, my Lord, to Thee,
I know no light, no hope, no peace
Apart from Thee, apart from Thee;
And so I come, my Lord, to Thee,
And find my way, my aim, my goal
In Thee, my God, in thee, my God."

Had there ever really been another early morning not so very long ago in far-away New York, when all had been sheer emptiness and desolation? Oh, the grace of God!

Chapter 9

The Haven

"Glory and praise from thankful hearts to Thee arise,
Songs of rejoicing fill the air today!
For true Thy word, unfailing,
For all our need availing,
We march on to conquer, fearless of the fray."[1]

As my personal life passed through these radical changes, the dark clouds of growing hostilities were fast gathering over Europe, and it was only a matter of months, following my return, that England was at war with Germany.

On that very day, Mother left our London home for the last time, and was driven to Haytor, South Devon, where she was to spend the remainder of her life. Here I joined her the next day from where I had been staying in Milford-on-Sea.

Never can I forget my first glimpse of The Haven. As I entered the gate, a brilliant splash of colour met my gaze, a glorious array of blue aubretia and golden alyssum, lining a long path of crazy paving; beyond, a green hill rising gently towards the sky.

Drawing nearer, I saw the charming little house

1. To Sing Thy Praise, Book 1. Evelyn Booth-Clibborn.

with its softly rounded bay windows and a blue porch, covered with clusters of yellow roses. In front of the house was a small heart-shaped pond; at its back, a rich variety of colourful shrubs. The effect upon my long city-accustomed spirit with its visions of endless grey streets and hard, impersonal buildings was indescribable; and this was to be our home.

The Haven, loaned to my Mother through the great kindness of her friend, Lady Violet Wills, M.B.E., was situated half-way down a steep, stony and twisting lane, at the bottom of which was an old farm surrounded by pasture land. At the top of the incline were the spacious hills of Dartmoor, commanding a view of rich valleys below.

This was a far cry from Broadway, New York, with its excitements and multitudinous distractions; yet, it was just here, in this remote and isolated countryside, that God began to train and discipline the life so lately yielded to Him.

This peaceful existence, in spite of its charms, was not congenial to one who all her life had been used to the battle-front, but Mother soon became immersed in what she called her "Pen Mission"; and there were always the visitors who either brought news or revived old memories. Her able secretary, who had travelled with her on her campaigns during the latter years, left at the outbreak of war to take up other work. A young woman, who proved a devoted and valuable helper, joined our little family at The Haven.

The great campaigns were over. There were to be a few sorties following the War, among them two tours of Scotland. Mother and I visited Switzerland, where, at each of her entries into packed halls and churches, the whole congregation would rise to its feet in silent tribute.

So God, in His goodness and mercy, allowed me to have this moving experience, as well as the privilege of assisting her once more at the piano. How could I express my joy at the restoration of an opportunity once lost!

Later, when journeys and meetings had ceased altogether, it was specially precious to hear Mother say, "I am glad you are with me, Evelyn, and that I am not alone".

To have brought her some cheer, and an added sense of security, was more than I could have hoped for, or ever deserved. But God was gently, almost imperceptibly, moving us towards the end of those sweet and comparatively calm years in the country. The war was fast receding into the past, Dame Violet Wills had already gone to live at her other residence in Clevedon, and Mother was drawing near to the close of a most remarkable life.

It was then that I put down a few of her prayers. They were always short and to the point. These are two of them:

"Lord, we thank you that you are not changeable. Keep us, O, keep us from going astray. Keep us true to Thy name, true to Thy purpose, true to Thy mission. Amen."

"Lord Jesus, if it please Thee, let us glorify Thee. Bless the letters I have sent out, that when they receive them they will say, 'I must DO something for Christ'."

Ever the practical Christian, this stands out in her second prayer. Almost to the end of her life (she died in her ninety-seventh year), this warrior of the cross would dress, come down for lunch and take a turn around the garden. The flame God had lit in her soul at a very early age never went out. This accounted for a basic determination not to give in, and even more for an overriding sense of urgency regarding Christ and His cause.

Two striking illustrations of this come to mind, one when Mother was about ninety-three. She had been lying on her bed, perfectly still, when she suddenly sat up, her eyes flashing, her voice as strong as ever. "Evelyn," she called to me, "when you get to my time of life you will see nothing in this world matters but what you have done for Jesus."

These words were all the more remarkable coming from one who had had a family of ten children, had contacted some of the most eminent people of her day, had travelled thousands of miles by land and sea, and had visited many of the world's most important cities.

The second incident occurred about three days before her death. I had been singing a little chorus of which she was very fond. It was a happy refrain about heaven.

"Do you want to go?" I asked her.

"No," came the firm reply. Then her voice broke, I want to see **THOUSANDS** come to Jesus."

How could she bear the thought of enjoying heaven, when countless millions were in outer darkness? God knew of that fire, of the burning desire to get them in. In His love for His child,

He took her while she was deeply unconscious, with double pneumonia. The doctor had remarked that her blood pressure and pulse were those of a young woman; nevertheless, he had warned me that she could succumb to the pneumonia.

My sister, Josephine, was with me at the end. It was in the month of May. Soon after our beloved Mother's promotion to glory, the dawn chorus broke the silence of the night, filling the air with ecstatic song. How fitting this seemed, as if heralding the joyous entry of God's devoted servant into the light of eternal day!

Chapter 10

Green Pastures

"To God I give the shining
Of steel-like faith and strong;
To God, the slow refining
Of heart and life and song.
That all to Him be given,
Of hopes, of joys, of pains;
That all to him be given,
Till nothing mine remains."[1]

Often when speaking in public, I have sought to describe Adèle, the quiet and humble Frenchwoman, who was led to give her whole life to our family, first as Nanny, and then as general helper.

That she should have been so used of God, on my behalf, was all the more remarkable because of the long separation. Yet, as far as our relationship was concerned, all that had occurred in between was as if it had never been; a signal mark, I felt, of God's over-ruling providence. He knew that, though I had been wonderfully restored, my need was very great and of a kind that perhaps only such a person, at such a time, could have met.

I had known the brilliance, sophistication and

1. To Sing Thy Praise, Book 1. Evelyn Booth-Clibborn.

restlessness of a large city, the strain of difficult friendships, and the inevitable drain of an exacting career, in both its performing and creative aspects. The utter simplicity, serenity and contentment of one of His lowliest servants was as "green pastures and still waters" to this tense but seeking disciple.

To come into her bedroom and quietly sit by her side was to be both healed and restored. There was no oppressiveness, as would have been the case with a false piety. On the contrary, I always felt a lift, a lightening of the spirit. For any fear or strain, there was invariably a quiet, assured word based on her knowledge of God. Most precious of all was her encouragement. I would read her a long letter written in French to a young convert, on which I had spent a great deal of time.

When I reached the end of it, her face would light up. "Oh!" she would exclaim, "she will be glad to receive that letter!"

To one longing to learn anew how to serve God, those words were wonderfully reassuring.

The kitchen was no less inspiring than the bedroom, for it was here that Adèle spent most of her days. That same lift would be felt on entering this room, and it was right here that the love and joy of home seemed most apparent.

My dear Mother, too, would relax from her beloved "Pen Mission" upstairs, and we would be a happy little family in our bright kitchen-diner, with its restful view of the garden. Mini, our little tabby cat, added to the precious sense of peace and well-being. This was an important part of God's loving reinstatement of His prodigal. I had never known the sense of home in the States.

There was also another side to this new existence. I had never before lived in the country, having only visited it on brief occasions. The fresh, clean air, the bird and animal life, the rural scenes with their soft, green pasture-land, winding lanes and rambling farm-houses were wholly enchanting.

This was the beginning of His way in my wilderness. Gradually, I began to realise that we were part of a little community. There were other houses owned by Dame Violet, which were situated along a private road at the top of the hill. These had been lent, by our kind and generous friend, to retired missionaries and others who had served God in various capacities.

On Sunday afternoons we would gather in the little meeting-room on that same private road, for Bible-studies and hymn-singing to the accompaniment of a small organ. Some years later, it fell to me to be responsible for these gatherings and to conduct the Bible-studies. Never had I been so challenged as when I began, week by week, to prepare these messages, and to discover the fascination of such study.

It was with very real regret that I had to relinquish these meetings upon leaving Haytor; but they had actually introduced me to a type of ministry with which I was to become more and more familiar. My Father was renowned among Christians on the continent of Europe (where he and my Mother laboured for so many years) for his deep teaching on spiritual matters, and perhaps it is from him I inherited a special love for this type of work.

For us in this peaceful setting, the war years passed without any outstanding incidents. We were still using Aladdin lamps and candles, electricity not yet having been installed; and all about us were familiar country sounds of the bleating of sheep and the soft lowing of deep-russet Devonshire cows.

The only exception to this calm was on the night of a devastating raid on Plymouth, twenty-five miles away, when, from the height of the nearby moors, I saw in the distance an angry red sky, and heard the repeated low booming of the bombs.

Those moors, how I loved them! Many a time, when assailed by doubts or some form of depression, I would climb up our long, stony lane onto the hills so close at hand, and pray as I walked along the grassy paths that, before going down again, God would lift the cloud from my soul; and how often He answered that prayer! It was during those times that the following hymn became so meaningful to me, and to this day, my spirit lifts at the very thought of these words.

"I would commune with Thee, my God,
And to Thy seat I come;
I leave my joys, I leave my sins
And seek in Thee my home.

I stand upon the mount of God
With sunshine in my soul:
I see the storms in vales beneath,
I hear the thunder's roll;

But I am calm with Thee, my God,
Beneath these glorious skies,
And to the height on which I stand
Nor storm nor clouds can rise.

Oh, this is life! O, this is joy!
My God, to find Thee so;
Thy face to see, Thy voice to hear;
And all Thy love to know!"[2]

Into the midst of this most happy time, came a severe blow. For the first time in my life, I found myself deeply in love with a Christian man who loved me and wanted to help me in the Lord's work. There were other influences in his life, however, not in sympathy with this new development, but directed towards other goals.

This resulted in a spiritual and emotional conflict in which I had no part, the Lord giving me no freedom to interfere. There was no question of forcing an issue, even though we were formally engaged. How could there be, when I had decided (that early morning in New York) that my life from then on was to be His way alone? All things, including this matter, were in His hands, not mine. But oh the cost of this isolated position!

Whilst I had known guilt, fear and torment, this was none of these things. What I now experienced was grief, just grief; but it was pure grief, for God was in it with me, and there was no bitterness. As I moved towards the end of this dark tunnel, light began to stream in, His light, which finally dispelled all darkness, leaving me clothed in a shining, God-given victory.

If leaving America was in a sense a coming out of Egypt, this particular episode was like a coming into Canaan, into a new spiritual stability and strength. It was an inner triumph of the Holy Spirit over the downward and debilitating pull of

2. 1200 Sacred Songs and Solos, no. 502. Ira D. Sankey.

grief; and confirmed that my dedication to God was unbroken and complete.

The last words of the hymn which opens this chapter expresses it all:

"Till losing self in giving,
I shall but see His plan
Absorbing all my living,
Outlasting all my span;
I shall but see His leading
As vanished days I view,
His patient, perfect leading
While making all things new."[3]

3. To Sing Thy Praise, Book 1. Evelyn Booth-Clibborn.

Chapter 11

My First Challenge

"God is enough, Oh, to live out this truth!
Life without Him has no worth.
God is enough, in Him all things are mine.
All things in heaven and earth!"[1]

The repercussions in other lives of these God-given victories were strong and unmistakable. Is it that the depth in one soul speaks to the depth in another? *"Deep calleth unto deep . . ."* (Psalm 42:7) seems to suggest this.

In spite of the very personal, almost private aspect of life in that rather remote part of Devon, outside activities were already claiming some of my time and involving me in journeys to different parts of England.

It was in about 1940 that an invitation came for me to spend a week with one of Mother's friends who lived in Bath. This lady kindly met me at the station upon my arrival, but no sooner were we seated together in her car, than she began to complain bitterly about her daughter.

It appeared that Hope had alienated herself from God, and her critical attitude was destroying all possibility of peace in the home. She frequented

1. To Sing Thy Praise, Book 2. Evelyn Booth-Clibborn.

the local public houses, and would often return in the small hours of the morning.

As I sat listening to Mother's friend, who was to me a complete stranger, I knew at once that God had a special purpose in bringing me into such an unhappy situation. Any thought of a possible rest (which had been the whole point of the visit) vanished instantly, and clear as noonday was the challenge which now faced me.

It was an attractive home. Mrs. B. (a widow), the daughter, and the maid were the only occupants. That evening, Hope, who worked for the near-by Admiralty, driving Army lorries, arrived back in time for dinner. I had been warned in advance by Mrs. B. about her daughter's antagonistic attitude towards her mother's 'religious' friends; so, at table, I gave almost my entire attention to the mother.

Evening after evening I would discourse upon the books I had read, the people and situations I had encountered during my travels, and the diverse experiences which had been part of my musical career. Not once did I make any reference to spiritual matters.

After a day or two, Mrs. B. told me privately with much excitement that she thought her daughter was really impressed with me, or words to that effect. Knowing that the coming Sunday would be my last Sunday with them, and that the daughter would be at home, I suggested to her mother that she should remark to her very casually that I enjoyed walking in the countryside.

Saturday came and, that evening, I was arranging my hair, standing in my bedroom, with my back to the door, which I taken good care to leave open. I knew the instant Hope had entered the room, though I could not see her and her tread was very light. "Miss Booth-Clibborn . . ." Her tone was so soft (so hard when she addressed her mother), almost unrecognisable.

"Yes," I said lightly, turning towards her.

"Miss Booth-Clibborn . . ." still the shyness, the diffidence. "Tomorrow will be Sunday," she continued, the words seeming to come with difficulty. "I wondered whether you would like to take a walk with me then?"

"Yes, I would, very much," I answered brightly, but with no sign of urgency, as I turned back to my hair-dressing.

Sunday was a day of brilliant sunshine, and, in the afternoon, we started out on our walk. We began climbing one of the many hills surrounding the old town, drinking in the lovely clear air. No word was spoken and the silence seemed to become more and more oppressive.

Suddenly, I said, "I believe there is something on your mind. Am I right?"

Then it came, a veritable flood of words, spoken in great bitterness of spirit. Her education had been wrong, her parents had been wrong; all their moving about from place to place had been wrong. I was to find that there had been some considerable truth in all this. On and on it flowed, that torrent of pent-up emotion, and I let it flow until it was completely exhausted.

By this time, we had reached the top of the hill and were sitting under a tree. There was a moment of silence; then I said, "You know I came to a similar dead-end myself."

"You?" Her tone was one of utter incredulity.

"Yes, I, too," I said quietly; "you see, I had chosen my way, friendships, occupations and musical career. I had had great light, but had allowed myself to drift in these different directions. Then in a moment of desperate need, when I became aware of the darkness and emptiness of my spiritual life, I began to seek God, but found that I had completely lost touch with Him."

I told her how, after the deepest remorse and a persistent search for Him, God spoke to me through His word, and how then and there I yielded my life to Him, an act which changed the whole course of that life.

Hope was looking down as I finished, and I can see now the two heavy drops of tears which fell on her lap. I then prayed quietly and briefly, affirming His love, grace and sufficiency, and we began to walk down the hill. No word was spoken; neither did I seek to break the silence. It was a very different silence from that which had preceded our talk.

That evening, after tea, to which she had invited a Christian lady (for my sake, I was told later), I sat down at the piano and played a hymn of my Father's. It was the first time I had done this, but the ice was now broken. I then played one of my own hymns, "O restless soul, dost thou not see God's great provision made for thee?"

Suddenly, Hope rose to her feet, and, with her handkerchief pressed to her mouth, hurried out of the room. Then something else took my attention. Her friend, too, had been deeply shaken and was weeping silently. I stopped playing. This was of the Holy Spirit. Softly I went over to that young woman, and we were able to talk over and commit to God a matter which had greatly troubled her.

As I was leaving the room, Mrs. B. rushed up to me in great agitation. "It's too late now," she said. Hope has gone off to do fire-service, and she leaves early for work in the morning."

After a moment's thought, I said, "Mrs. B., would you get me a pencil and paper?"

She hurried off to find them, returning almost immediately. "Dear Hope," I wrote, "you know I wake quite early. If you would like to say goodbye before you go to work, I shall be delighted. If not, I shall quite understand. In any case, thanks for a happy time."

That, in substance, was the note I sent her. My very desire to be awake early the following morning must have acted on my subconscious; or was it the Lord Himself, so in control of the situation, who alerted me to being on time? Be that as it may, I was awake long before it was necessary, waiting, praying and listening. Then I heard it, that little timid knock on the door. "Come in," I said brightly, and in she came.

Dressed and ready for work, she walked briskly towards my bed, and began to talk in a bright and breezy manner. Suddenly, I knew that it was now or never. "Hope," I said gently, "did you want to come back to Christ?"

Her reaction was extreme and unmistakable, for she literally fell by my bed, her very body seeming to bear her inner load of misery, and sobbed as if her heart would break.

As she wept, I prayed aloud for her in words which I felt we should both say to the Lord: how hard we were by nature; how rebellious and proud in our independence; how deeply sorry we were for all this, and how deeply unhappy because of it. Gently, so gently, we came to the feet of our Saviour, asking His forgiveness, offering ourselves afresh, just as we were, to be His for ever.

Then I said quietly, "You, too, Hope, must speak to Him, telling Him how sorry you are, how you are coming back to Him with all your heart, never to leave Him again." This she did in utter simplicity and with deepest contrition, and rose to her feet free from the intolerable burden she had borne for so long.

Soon after my return to The Haven, I received a letter from her mother, who wrote, "My home is now a heaven". Hope never looked back and one of her earliest requests was that I should sing and speak to her friends in their drawing room, "even as you did to me". This was the very first Recital-Talk, a combination of music and testimony, I ever gave.

Hope never lost her burning desire to bring others to Christ, often asking me to minister to them in some way or another. Although she was eventually to die of Multiple Sclerosis, I never once heard her complain. All this does not mean that this particular Christian did not have the weaknesses and failures common to human nature. She had her share. But her love for the Lord never weakened from that early morning in Bath to the end of her life.

Chapter 12

Called to Personal Ministry

"God is ever true; I know that
God is ever true;
I can rest upon His promise,
I can trust His every word,
Knowing that
God is ever true."[1]

There are sudden and unusual experiences that can challenge the very quality of our faith. The following incident did just this for me, and, at the same time, revealed Christ's all-sufficiency.

This intensely personal ministry, to which God seemed to be calling me, continued. Indeed, sometimes it met me right at the Haven itself.

One day, upon opening the door of our home, I came face to face with a spectacle of ruin. The appearance of the woman standing before me was quite frightening in its gaunt and tragic aspect. Instinctively, I felt that here was something deeply and terribly wrong. My mother, who had invited the person for a visit but had not realised how extreme was the situation, asked me if I would undertake for our guest.

Such a degree of human suffering seemed almost

1. To Sing thy Praise, Book 2. Evelyn Booth-Clibborn

an intrusion into the quiet life we led at that time; and I very soon realised that only a total involvement on my part, as God's instrument, could possibly meet the problem. Even so, it was a daunting prospect. Through the unrelenting mental cruelty of another, this person had been robbed of all confidence, all capacity to feel, and all interest in life. Whatever note was struck gained no response at all. But there could be no by-passing the issue. It was to be all or nothing; complete victory or total defeat.

What walks we took together over the heights and slopes of Dartmoor. How wonderfully God led His servant to touch on the lighter themes, often funny and merry ones, as we trod the grassy paths hither and thither.

Then came the first glimmerings of light breaking through those heavy clouds of oppression; and her laughter, unbelievable at first, yet unmistakable, broke the terrible tension of many days.

Still the walks went on, love and laughter alone doing their healing and restoring work, while all the serious subjects were carefully avoided. Indeed, so light was the spiritual touch, it could hardly have been detected. Yet how blessedly effective it proved.

One day, when sitting together indoors, the inner waters which had been steadily rising in her soul, burst their banks, in a flood of tears. Oh, the blessedness of those tears! The poison was released. Now at last could come the "binding of the wounds" and the "pouring in of oil and wine". Christ's love, forgiveness and healing were to be deeply absorbed by one who, for so long, had known no love, no forgiveness and no healing.

She left our home completely restored and in radiant health to start a new task for her Lord.

Her letters again and again testified of her great joy and of her deepest gratitude to God for His unfailing love and mercy.

Another account of how God overruled circumstances, bringing His own purposes to pass, is of a very different character.

In 1943, during one of my visits to London, I received a letter which greatly disturbed me. At the time I was assisting at a women's meeting in what was then the Mildmay Centre. With my many commitments, I had completely forgotten to answer a letter from a woman who had written to me expressing a deep desire to adopt a little girl. My negligence distressed me. A friend had asked if I could help this person, who was married but with no children. I got in touch with her immediately, and the next thing I remember is the two of us earnestly discussing the matter on the top of a London bus. Since she was already in middle life, she naturally would prefer the little girl to be not less than five years of age.

When we arrived back at the Mildmay Centre, I took her up to my room where we could continue our conversation without interruption. From what I could gather, she had made no specific commitment to Christ, though was a very honest and good-living woman. I felt, in fairness to all three of us, the child, the adult and myself, that I should make quite clear the only basis on which I could act on her behalf.

"You know I want to help you," I said, "but it would not be right for me to go and find a little girl for you unless we had prayed about it. How else would I know that she was the right child for you or you the right mother for the child?"

So we knelt there together in that large, cold room, committing this strange, unknown venture into the hands of God. Then it was that I took the plunge, but not without some trepidation. Had I the right to ask the question I was about to put to her?

"If the Lord should indeed give you a little girl," I said very gently, "would you be willing to give her back to the Lord, even as Hannah did Samuel?"

"Yes I would," she said just as quietly.

This simple straightforward answer rebuked and humbled me, condemning such doubts I may have had. It was a further sign of God's undertaking. After that I knew the way was clear for Him to lead me to the child of His choice.

The next day I had to leave for Bristol, and it was there I began my enquiries. Having discovered where the necessary information could be obtained, I soon found myself in a small room with a rather formidable-looking person seated at a table, with a large book in front of her.

Having explained the circumstances of my friend, I said that she would like to adopt a little girl not less than five years old. The amazement of the social-worker almost bordered on anger. To want a babe or infant, that was understandable, but a child of five! Suddenly she began turning the pages of her book. "Well, there is just one . . .", the words came abruptly, "only one of that age, and she cannot be returned once she has been taken", she added warningly. "We have stopped all that; it has caused far too much trouble."

How could she know the sense of wonder I

felt. I had placed the matter in God's hands. So this, the only child of that age, must be the one! Peace filled my heart.

When the would-be mother went to see this little girl in a Home for Child Care, she was startled by her appearance. Her hair was cut close to her head, her eyes were covered with styes, and she uttered not a word in response to her visitor's warm and gentle approach. Yet the mother-heart took her, just as she was. There was never the slightest regret in having done so. Indeed, joy is the keynote of that entire story.

And what a welcome awaited the intensely shy and lonely child. A hot bath and a warm bed were in readiness, not to mention two hearts only too eager to give her all the love and care she needed.

It was over ten years — except for one brief meeting soon after her adoption —before I saw Evelyn (her new name) again. Evelyn was then a sweet girl of sixteen. She had just given her heart to the Lord. Her mother had written to me, telling me that right from the start, her daughter had loved going to Sunday School at a near-by Baptist Chapel. This undoubtedly paved the way for her conversion.

But there was more to come. As the mother walked with me to the Underground station, she spoke a little about herself. "When I adopted Evelyn," she said, "I felt that I should begin to attend a church. This I did and have continued to do so regularly. It was at this Baptist Chapel that I too became a Christian."

Only one thing would I add to this brief

account of what covered many years. Some time later, Evelyn married a good Christian man. The marriage has been a very happy one, and both are attending and supporting a nearby Evangelical Church.

Chapter 13

God-Given Victory

"Thine the word that set me free,
Shedding light into my gloom;
All my life must sing to Thee,
All my being give Thee room;
Songs and words and work and play,
All to Thee must point the way."[1]

At last came the day when we were to say good-bye to The Haven, our much-loved country home and scene of so many dear and unforgettable memories. Since Mother — for whom we had come there in the first place — was no longer with us, it seemed impracticable to remain in so isolated a location, especially with my growing commitments away from home.

But it was a sad time, that latter part of 1957, with its seeming break-up of what had been such a happy little family. Our beloved Adèle was to be cared for in turn by my sister, Josephine, and my brother, Theodore, and Mother's devoted helper was to live near her brother in Haytor. My own path was still obscure, though by that time I knew I was to go to Bournemouth.

Praying much for guidance as to where God

1. To Sing Thy Praise, Book 1. Evelyn Booth-Clibborn.

actually wanted me to live, I eventually called at Slavanka, a Conference Centre in Bournemouth, where I had previously visited with Mother. Mr. Allan, the manager at the time, gave me an immediate and very warm welcome, should I want to make my home with them. As I sat in the lounge, I had an unusual sense of peace, which I again experienced shortly after my arrival, while sitting on the cliffs, viewing the Bournemouth coastline. My heart was full of gratitude for God's hand in having brought me to my destination. Slavanka was to be my home; the scene of much activity in the Lord's service, and base for my journeys and engagements in His Name.

I was privileged, as opportunities arose, to assist in the work of the Girl Crusaders' Union, an inter-denominational movement dedicated to Bible teaching among schoolgirls, whose General Secretary, Miss Isobel Macdonald, I had come to know some years earlier.

Much of my work has been with youth. Time and again, the Spirit would break through any fear or resistance in a young life; and, melting it completely, would create a new, tender and submissive spirit.

Very often, in stressing the death to self — "not I, but Christ" — principle, there can come a false restraint, which is not of the Spirit. Oh, the eagerness of many a girl and leader, both to know and see such vitality that is born of the Spirit! What joy they felt and expressed on discovering that the Lord could use and transform whatever natural gifts they had! One of my Mother's sayings was, "God uses — not crushes — personality".

I remember many a golden August at Aberlour camp in the north of Scotland; especially the

Sunday evening hymn-singing, led by Miss Macdonald, when our worship would often include this favourite from the Scottish Psalter:

"I to the hills will lift mine eyes . . ."

and, as we sang, the view from the window of those glorious Spey-side hills lent its own inspiration.

At St. Margaret's camp in Shropshire, there was a real touch of revival, and one girl told her leader some years later, "It was the turning point of my life".

What remains so clearly in my mind, from when I spoke at Stover School, Devon, is the impact of the Holy Spirit upon that gathering. After the meeting, I walked towards the room where coffee was to be served; but to my surprise, it was empty except for one young woman, seated in the centre of it, weeping bitterly. The commandant saw in a moment what was happening, and decided to have refreshments in another room. Feeling free to approach her, I gently asked her what the matter was.

"I am a failure," she cried. "I have failed as a Christian and as a teacher."

I did not interrupt the flood of tears but simply said, "It is good that God has shown you this and that your heart is tender and repentant before the Lord. That is where we all begin, acknowledging our own unworthiness and utter helplessness apart from Him." She began to quieten down and was listening. "Repentance is good and essential," I continued, "but you are not going to stay there, looking at your failure. There are two sides in the Christian life: Defeat and Victory. So let us claim the victory now."

This we did as we knelt together, and she went

out radiant with a strong, renewed faith in her Lord and His all-sufficiency.

This is the power of the Word:

"Thanks be to God who gives us the victory through our Lord Jesus Christ." (1 Corinthians 15:57).

Chapter 14

Battles Won!

"All glory to God and to Jesus the Son,
Who by the blest Spirit our battle has won,
And ended for us all that love had begun
Hallelujah, hallelujah, hallelujah, Amen."[1]

"Thanks be to God who gives us the victory through our Lord Jesus Christ." (1 Corinthians 15:57).

Little did I know how significant that verse was to become in my ministry for the Lord. Perhaps in His dealings with those who are more mature, have deeper problems, know stronger temptations, God reveals an even greater manifestation of His power.

That first Recital-Talk, given for Hope and her friends in Bath, laid down a pattern for meetings in many and varied places. This combination of music and testimony was graciously used by God in bringing many to a knowledge of salvation, and to a deeper commitment in His service. I would play classical pieces, followed by some of my hymns and choruses; then I would speak of the Lord's dealings in my life, based upon His word.

Following a Recital-Talk in a friend's large and

1. To Sing Thy Praise, Book 1. Evelyn Booth-Clibborn.

beautiful drawing-room, when most of the guests had left, I found myself face to face with a young woman I shall call Joan. She was the very person my friend had been anxious I should speak to alone, and this seemed a God-given opportunity.

I believe I must have asked her whether she was a Christian, for her answer came readily enough, a bitter one, "I've tried again and again to be a Christian," she said, "but without success."

"Yes," I said, "and you can go on trying but you will never become one. That is not the way to become a Christian. Do you think you can achieve what it cost the life-blood of the Son of God to make you?"

We were standing on either side of the grand piano on which I had lately played, and Joan lit a cigarette and began pacing backwards and forwards. This was the beginning of a long talk which lasted well into the night. When at last we knelt to pray, she rose suddenly to her feet saying, "I am not ready for that."

"All right," I said quietly, "I can wait. Time does not matter."

When around midnight we knelt again to pray, the battle was won. The spirit of the antagonist had become the spirit of a little child, as Joan in deep humility received Jesus Christ into her life as her Lord and Saviour.

The next morning early, before I was up, came a knock on my door. It was Joan. After greeting me, she went and stood looking out of the window. "All my life," she said, "I have lived in a fog. But not any longer. Next Sunday I shall go to Communion."

Sometimes, however, the influence of the enemy

is so entrenched in a person that it might take much longer for a spiritual victory to be won.

Not so long after my arrival at Slavanka, I met a very successful nurse whom I shall call Sylvia. She loved the children it was her joy to serve. Had she not given her life to nursing them? And how her love was returned, their faces lighting up whenever she entered the room. It was a wonderful gift which Sylvia gave unreservedly to her little patients.

She had a very lively, confident and attractive personality. Who would have dreamt that she had suffered two tragedies in her life which had left deep tracks of fear and bitterness? They had been carefully covered by that bright, sparkling surface. Her manner was so warm and engaging that many took for granted that she was a Christian.

But it was soon clear to me that all was not well with her. At the same time came the knowledge that God was laying a burden on my heart for this person.

As soon as Sylvia sensed my concern for her, the battle was on. My tentative approach had been as if a fuse had touched some inner, inflammable matter, causing a minor explosion.

"Be careful of Miss Booth-Clibborn," said someone laughingly, "she converts people!"

"No flies on me!" was the swift reply.

That was March 7th, 1958. The battle went on, and Sylvia would return to Slavanka when free. It was as if, in spite of herself, she sensed just how desperate was her need. I think it will be simpler to quote from my diary.

March 8th. and 9th. Sylvia in great inner turmoil and conflict. Her whole attitude one of rebellion because of past years. Her fiancé, a Group Captain in the war, had been killed in action.

March 10th. Prayed together. Believe on.

June 27th. and 30th. Very difficult times with Sylvia. Only partial deliverance, then back into the same spirit of rebellion. Praying and believing.

Sept. 28th. Sylvia again under a heavy cloud. Up most of the night with her. Believe on.

Sept./Oct. Saw Sylvia two or three times. Still very unsettled.

A whole year passed, then on November 5th, 1959, at 9.30 p.m., Sylvia came up to my room. She was still very overwrought. After a while, she said very softly,

"I am ready to come to Him."

We came to Him together, and I later claimed the precious blood to cover her.

When Sylvia at last came through into peace, it was a complete victory, because it was His victory, not hers; and she was not slow in testifying to this.

On November 19th, arriving back at Slavanka from an engagement, I found Sylvia already there. During my absence, she had been talking to senior workers in the house. "Miss Booth-Clibborn told me the truth about myself," she said, "and every time she did, I hated her more. But that's all over. I've come to the Lord."

Afterwards, I received a long and

wonderful letter from Sylvia, covering that whole period from March 1958 to November 1959. Repeatedly, her words were in this vein,

"It was your **Love** (God's **Love** in and through me) that never failed."

Chapter 15

Recital-Talks

"There is a joy that comes unsought
When we the cross embrace,
A deeper joy than we had thought
Could spring alone from grace.

Yet grace abounding is the source
That sweetens all its ways;
And no obstruction stays its course;
It sings and sings His praise!

It flows on deep within the heart,
Its waters fresh and clear;
With fears and doubts it has no part;
They may not come too near.

O joy that sweetens toil and pain!
A gift of love and grace!
O sparkling, ever new refrain,
Bright'ning the darkest place!"[1]

If I felt that the Recital-Talk in the parish hall of St. John's Church, Boscombe, was a Recital-Talk with a difference, there were further developments to come in the years ahead.

1. To Sing thy Praise, Book 2. Evelyn Booth-Clibborn.

It was a special delight to work with Rev. Gordon Guinness, because I had known the family over many years, and had helped his wife with women's meetings. Rev. Guinness sat on the platform with me during the piano recital, and the music was interspersed with questions and answers about my faith and ministry, rather in the nature of an arm-chair debate.

While enjoying this informality, I was not to know how unusually the Spirit would lead me at the end of the evening. As the people crowded into the passage leading to the exit, my attention was drawn to a young man who, as it happened, was looking straight at me. "Are you a Christian?" I called.

"No," came the prompt reply.

"Would you like to be?"

"Yes."

"Then come to my hotel tomorrow morning," I said, giving the name and address.

I should explain that there was no privacy for counselling. This was a severe test for me. Would he come? Had I lost an opportunity? It would be so easy for him to change his mind and not turn up. But he came.

He was a Chinese boy, fresh-faced and clear-eyed, his very earnestness showing the influence of the vicar's God-given messages. We went into the hotel lounge and after a few introductory words, I explained to him the way of salvation. Nelson's response to Christ, when he received Him as his own Saviour and Lord, was among the clearest and most definite I have ever heard. His letter following that memorable morning, was a confirmation of his total committal to God. "As I left the hotel," he wrote, "the trees were new, the sky was new, God was new!"

Nelson was asked to give his testimony in one of the tents at the Keswick Convention, and not long after, he entered the Cirencester College, where he led his room-mate to the Lord.

Some time later, I received a letter from him written on the ship that was taking him back to China. He was returning because he could not get a job in England. This was a real shock to me and I replied at once. "Why did you not write to me? I would have helped you to get work."

His answer, coming from one so young in the faith, humbled me to the earth. "I felt, like St. Paul, that I should *not consult with flesh and blood.*" (Galatians 1:16). He was right; I was wrong.

As soon as Nelson arrived back in China, relatives tried to get him married to a Chinese girl. But he refused to agree to this plan as she was not a Christian. He did eventually marry a Christian girl, and he took a position in a university.

Much more recently a friend of mine received a letter from Nelson saying, "I have decided that whatever God does, and whatever God does not do . . . is right for my family. In any event, I will trust Him." Nothing could describe the joy those words brought me, because it showed that Nelson and his family were going on with the Lord.

Towards the end of the fifties, I prepared a brochure describing my Recital-Talks. One of the results of this was an invitation from an inter-denominational committee to hold three such meetings in Belfast, which I took as a definite leading from the Lord to develop my ministry along these lines.

The undue formality of the first, to which only bankers and their wives had been invited, restrained me from speaking at any depth about the Lord's dealings with my life. Even the grand piano was stiff to my touch. I could not go much beyond narrating the bare facts of my musical career, my début as a concert artist, and my eventual turning to God in total dedication. Yet was it not the Spirit who prompted me to play Bach's 'Jesu, Joy of Man's Desiring'?

The second was a complete contrast to the first. It was characterised by a much warmer and freer atmosphere. God's touch is always right, no matter whether the gathering is formal or informal.

For the third, a Christian dental surgeon booked a hotel room as the venue. He had invited his professional friends to dinner, to be followed by the Recital-Talk. I was to have my meal apart, in one of the hotel rooms. How the Lord blessed my solitary prayer-time. It was an earnest of the blessing to come.

Earlier, as we were approaching the hotel, my host, extremely nervous, had said, "You will play a lot, won't you?" I was very touched, sensing the big step of faith he was taking.

I do not remember the actual message I gave, but the impact of the Holy Spirit upon me was unforgettable. I was borne along with great power, and as I finished speaking, a Christian lady flung her arms around me, her face radiant with joy.

God does not always give visible 'signs following'. Four years passed before I heard of two young Christian women, who, having drifted very far into the world, came right back to Christ through those Recital-Talks.

Chapter 16

"Hymns My Soul Would Raise!"

"Music fills my heart today,
Sweet refrains of love and joy!
For Thou, Lord, dost lead the way,
Thine the strength none can destroy;
Thine the glory, Thine the praise,
These the hymns my soul would raise!"[1]

"Did you write the hymn:

'All that I need, all that I need,
Jesus, dear Lord, Thou art all that I need'?"[2]

The question was put to me suddenly by a fellow-musician, while I was still preoccupied with my musical career. It was as if I heard the distant sound of a church bell borne across the clamour of a large city.

My reply came readily enough. Yes, I had written that hymn some years back. How is it that I should have expressed such a deep truth when I was not following the Lord? Certainly,

1. To Sing Thy Praise, Book 1. Evelyn Booth-Clibborn.

2. To Sing Thy Praise, Book 1. Evelyn Booth-Clibborn

there were moments of revelation from God, even though I was 'afar off'. Had I not amazingly experienced His glory, while working in the filing department of that New York bank?

At the time of crisis in New York, when the Lord spoke so unmistakably to me, alone in my room, I knew without a doubt that I had allowed God no part in my music. Yet had He not, in a moment of intense depression, given me, as direct from Himself, that chorus: 'All power have I'?

When I returned to England, I kept up my practice of classical pieces and greatly enjoyed performing these at Recital-Talks. Far from discouraging my musical talent, the Lord impressed upon me the significance of using it to His glory. At the Haven, I came across some verses that had been discarded. I changed the melodic line; but when I sang the verses to my Mother, she said, "That doesn't get anywhere. Why don't you write a chorus?"

I went immediately onto the tennis court, and once again a chorus was directly given to me. It fitted the verses as a glove a hand:

> **"So let us trust in the darkness,**
> **Let us not doubt any more,**
> **For with the morning comes Jesus,**
> **Jesus will stand on the shore."[3]**

During my early years at Slavanka, as I took morning prayers, I discovered the sheer joy of leading studies in Old Testament characters, such as Joseph, Nehemiah, Elijah and Esther, and others from the New Testament. This deeper ministry was being used increasingly at camps and

3. To Sing Thy Praise, Book 1. Evelyn Booth-Clibborn.

conferences. Therefore, I began to wonder whether God wanted me to concentrate more on Bible teaching than on evangelism.

It was at this point that a Recital-Talk had been arranged in the home of Michael and Pauline Young in Foxton, Cambridge. I ventured to 'put out a fleece' before the Lord. If He wanted me to continue with Recital-Talks, would He please win a soul to Himself that night.

The conversion which transformed Valerie M's life was God's answer to my prayer. That was in 1969, and was but the beginning of a warm and fruitful ministry, which has lasted twenty years, and still continues.

I need not have worried. No ministry can be too comprehensive. God was interweaving the expositions of Bible characters with the combination of music and testimony. At the same time, He was dealing with me personally at a profound level.

It may be significant to mention a vivid dream I had relating to the episode of falling in love, shortly after my return from America. It was the same situation, the same terrible ache. Fantastic, after twenty years. Fantastic, too, because of the continuing victory I had experienced over such a long period. Could it be that God allowed this dream to show how His victory towered above any hidden record of the subconscious? From all this, I was to go on to experience a surge of the Holy Spirit's power, the outcome of which was a harvest of souls.

From the mid-sixties until 1978, I was on the road, as it were. The hymns and choruses God had given me, and continued to give me, were published in two song-books: 'To Sing Thy Praise' nos. 1 and 2. I had earlier felt a strong leading to write down the testimony concerning my spiritual crisis and return to God; so that when it was suggested that I make a tape of it for the World Evangelisation Crusade, it needed only to be streamlined for the recording made in 1963. This has since been re-done on two cassettes, which as 'The Story behind the Songs', along with 'To Sing Thy Praise', have been sold on my travels, God graciously blessing what He gave to His glory. In 1966, I took three hundred copies of 'To Sing Thy Praise' no. 1 to America, and returned with only a handful.

A letter had come from Mrs. Johnson, the Christian friend who had bought a box at my concert début. and helped financially with my return to England. She was in her eighties, and going blind, and she had asked me if I would stay with her for three months in order to read to her and be her comapnion. All expenses met.

This meant the concellation of many engagements, but my friends were very understanding, knowing how exceedingly kind Mrs. Johnson had been to me during difficult times. God blessed that visit in showing how strong was my 'new life' in comparison with the 'old life' in that very same city of New York.

Chapter 17

Clutching Fingers

"Oh Christ, Thy call
Has now bound our hearts to Thee;
Forsaking all,
Thine and Thine alone to be,
We give our all
For Thy service glad and free.
In Thy name, we go,
Strong to meet the foe,
That Thy triumph all may see."[1]

There were many constraints on my movements, unexplained reactions to my ministry, unexpected personal disappointments. It was as if I had no liberty to come and go as I pleased. But if I was to be of any use to Him, I must accept the daily discipline of a surrendered will. I recall again the words of my Father's hymn:

"Wherever you ripe fields behold
Waving to God their sheaves of gold,
Be sure some corn of wheat has died,
Some saintly soul been crucified."

One invitation followed another to speak and

1. To Sing Thy Praise, Book 1. Evelyn Booth-Clibborn

play and sing for the Lord. When I did just that, the individual touch of the Spirit fell upon one here and one there, until often they were broken and weeping before the Lord.

I remember a gathering of young people where this very thing happened.

I had been speaking with a great sense of the Spirit upon me, when suddenly I became aware of a teen-age girl on the back row. Her face seemed utterly shattered.

She was already a Christian, but it was very evident that the Lord had spoken to her in a new way. She was transformed. A hunger had been created for the Lord which was insatiable. A lengthy correspondence ensued, in which she was eager to go ever deeper in the faith.

Since then she has married, her three children are all Christians, and she and her husband have started a Christian marriage guidance ministry.

Years before this, I witnessed the transformation of another life. The circumstances were different, but the willingness to give God all was the same.

This particular young person was an accomplished sportswoman whom I had occasion to challenge,

"What made you seek God?"

"My horse threw me, and I knew as I went through the air that I was not ready to meet God."

When I visited her after her conversion, the mantelpiece, formerly over-loaded with sporting trophies ("I was a queen when I walked onto the tennis court!") was empty. Her reply to my enquiry was,

"They just don't go with the Lord!"

I would like to share with you one message in

particular which seemed to be specially used by the Lord. It is the incident of the lad with the loaves and fish.

"Jesus went up into the mountain," we read in John chapter six, **"and there He sat with His disciples."** When He saw a great company coming towards Him, He asked Philip how they would find bread to feed the people. For everyone to have even a little, it would take more than two hundred pennyworth of bread, came the reply. Andrew then spoke up, **"There is a lad here who has five barley loaves and two small fish. But what are they among so many?"**

The world can never do with us what God can do. In spite of its progress in the study of man, it has neither the divine knowledge nor the divine power. It is God who chooses the weak things of the world to confound the mighty, because it is God alone who can do it. Man looks for learning, cleverness and personality. God, while not deprecating such human assets, looks for someone humble enough for Him to use.

"There is a lad here . . ." Where exactly was he? Since he was visible in spite of the crowd, he must have been somewhere near the front. How had this happened? Boys do not usually stay in one spot, nor do they normally mix with adults. He might have come out of curiosity because of what he had seen and heard of Christ, or he might have felt the love and grace of this wonderful Person. The fact that he brought loaves and fish with him would suggest that he was prepared to listen to the great Teacher.

One thing was certain, he was somewhere near Christ, where the divine presence could be felt, and contact was possible. Could this be the reason so many miss Him altogether? They never come near enough, either to see him or listen; and so, absorbed into the crowd, they gradually drift away and are lost.

We are not told that the Lord called the boy, but he could not have come unbidden. The conclusion would seem that Andrew went to fetch the lad, to bring him to Christ. If this is correct, it would be from the boy himself that Jesus took the loaves.

Let us consider what in the lad's own experience could have preceded such contact with Christ. We can imagine how closely he must have watched the Lord. He would see Him talking to one of His disciples who, when replying, would appear troubled and agitated. He would then observe another disciple approaching the Master to say something. Were they looking in his direction? They couldn't be! Then the impossible happened. That disciple was coming straight towards him. "Surely, he's not coming to me?" he would breathe, panic seizing him. "Yes, he is . . . he is . . . straight to me!"

We can then hear Andrew's quiet voice in the lad's ear telling him, "The Master has need of you," and, as the lad started back in fear, reassuring him, "I will go with you."

It might be good to pause here and remember the thousands of dedicated disciples who, through the years, have led some faltering person to Christ; and also to recall Jesus' words, **"I will make you fishers of men".**

The lad came face to face with the Lord. "He is putting out His hands for my loaves and fish.

But why? Can He not get anything He wants? All those miracles. Besides, I'm hungry, and this is my lunch. I know. I've five loaves. I'll give him three. He's already taken the two fish. I'll keep back two loaves. He won't miss them, and they mean a lot to me."

Do we not reason like that sometimes? Why should we given everything to Christ? Have we no rights of our own? What about clutching fingers? An incident comes to mind.

It was evening in the Children's Hospital. The skeleton staff moved about quietly, finishing their tasks before the night staff came to relieve them. Lights were dimmed in the ward as the little ones were being tucked in for the night. A senior nurse heard an impatient voice at her side, "Please, staff nurse, may I go now? I'm going to a dance tonight and I don't want to be late."

Suddenly, a plaintive cry was heard from half-way down the ward. "Nurse," said her superior, "will you first see who is crying and do what you can to soothe the child."

A frown crossed the nurse's face, and with a toss of the head she strode down the ward, muttering to herself, "I want to go. There are other people here who can do this. Anyway, this isn't my section."

"What is the matter, child?" she said, on reaching the cot, "Why don't you go to sleep?"

"I want my teddy."

"Well then, find your teddy."

The child sat up and, with her little hands, felt all around the bed, but in vain.

"Hurry up," the nurse said, not unkindly.

A big sob broke from the child, "Oh, it's gone, teddy's gone!"

The nurse bent down, found the teddy, and held it out. "Here it is. Now off to sleep with you."

The child stretched out her arms, gropingly to take the teddy; and then it was that the nurse saw that the child was blind. Quietly and gently, she put the treasured teddy into the outstretched arms. The little one hugged it to her, and a lovely smile spread over the tear-stained face. It was the nurse's eyes that were now filled with tears.

All through the dance, she told the staff nurse later, the child had been in her thoughts. When she had loosened her hold on that which she so wanted her heart had opened.

The lad held nothing back. When he opened his hands to give what he had to the Lord, could his heart have remained closed? Humble and inconspicuous, he moved into another world, a larger world, full of wonder, warmth and blessedness.

A hush had descended upon the crowd. The Lord Jesus was holding his gift and praying over it. That was only the beginning. He then began to give out the loaves and fish, and went on and on giving out. The people were all seated, five thousand of them, and the disciples kept coming back for more. Still the loaves and the fish seemed to pour out of his hands. It was incredible.

"That was my lunch; I gave it to Him." O, the wonder of it!

Yes, the lad was part of the divine plan, of that tide of blessing, of the miracle itself. The initial transaction between Christ and himself was passed. He now stood far in the background of that impressive scene, a small, very small part of something infinitely greater.

On and on went the flow of loaves and fish from the Master's hands, until the people had 'eaten their fill'; even so, there were twelve baskets-full of fragments left over. It was a great miracle; but it could not compare with that which it symbolised. Christ Himself, the living bread, is the divine food of countless multitudes; and that miracle, the greater miracle, has continued to this day, and will continue.

What would have happened if the lad had refused to give his loaves and fish to Christ? He would have stood there, still clutching them, just one of the crowd. The miracle would doubtless have taken place, with or without him, but he would not have been 'in the miracle'. He would have eaten the food provided by the miracle (such is the grace of God); but he would have had no part in the glorious plan itself.

As he drifted away with the crowd, that refuge of retreat, would there not have been an ache in his heart, a strange sense of emptiness?

Chapter 18

On the Move

"So, Lord, I would Thy love proclaim,
Thy risen life for all who seek
Forgiveness in the Saviour's name.
In that dear name, Lord let me speak."[1]

In 1975, I flew with Pauline Young, at her invitation, to Germany. Since we had learned German at home, I was able to speak at three meetings in Hamburg: one in a Baptist church, where three people were counselled; the other two in Hostenwall, where I gave a brief message during a Sunday morning service.

At a Recital-Talk held in the evening there was a lovely atmosphere; never shall I forget the joy and freedom I felt in speaking on *"Joseph is a fruitful bough"* (Genesis 49:22), which illustrates the blessed and visible outcome of a godly life. The Lord had put His own seal upon that visit, and Pauline and I had a deep sense of fulfilment and thanksgiving.

It was that same year, 1975, that my visits to the North West of England began. They were to continue for the next eleven years, covering a wide geographical area, and a variety of venues. Here

1. To Sing Thy Praise, Book 1. Evelyn Booth-Clibborn.

I quote from a letter received from one who found the Lord.

"Meeting you, and learning the meaning of true faith and peace, has helped so much through all the ups and downs of life during the past years; and knowing that God will sustain me, no matter what happens, is just too wonderful for words. Thank you for showing me the Way."

These many journeys were not without their touches of humour.

I had arrived by taxi at Euston station to catch a train for Manchester. No porter or trolley was in sight. When I expressed my concern to the taxi driver, he simply picked up my luggage and walked with me across the large concourse, accompanying me as far as the ticket office. As I stood at the top of a steep incline, leading to the platform, I knew that I could not possibly carry my luggage down to where the train was already waiting. Then, incredibly, the taxi driver was back. He picked up my luggage.

"You're a wonderful man," I said.

"I will tell my wife," was the quick reply.

The next thing I knew was that he was putting me and my luggage into the train just as it was starting to move.

It was a crowded smoking compartment, but I managed to find a seat beside a charming lady who turned out to be an interior decorator. Opposite us sat a young man with a lovely smile, called Joe.

"Would you like a cup of tea?" said the young lady to me.

"Oh, yes," I replied, "I would love one."

At this, Joe jumped up and was gone, only to

return with a steaming hot cup of tea and two cans of beer.

"I think you will need your coat," my thoughtful neighbour then suggested.

"I'll get it," said Joe, reaching up for the garment. As he pulled it down, everything came with it; the tea went, the beer went, and a small lake formed on the table. By this time, the atmosphere was free and warm. "I had a grandmother," Joe said. "She was dying, and I offered to sit with her for four nights. When it came to the fourth night, she suddenly cried, 'It's Jesus!' And was gone."

"Of course," I said, "she knew Him, and was ready for Him." My voice had risen as I spoke, and there was dead silence in the compartment.

Joe was embarrassed. "I don't go to church," he said.

"It doesn't matter whether you go to church or not," I replied. "If you were on a desert island, and called upon the name of Jesus, He would hear you and answer you."

We had arrived at Manchester. Nothing more was said. But the message had been given.

Mention has been made before of the touch of revival. This was to happen again during a visit I made to Clarendon School, on the eve of the fire, in September 1975. Even more significant was the fact that the Lord gave a similar outpouring of His Holy Spirit, when I visited the School a second time in its new quarters in Bedford. There were nineteen conversions and nine restored backsliders.

1981 was the Centenary of the Salvation Army — L'Armée du Salut — in France. Since Mother, known as the Maréchale, founded that work in 1881, I was asked whether I would represent the family on that occasion. This I considered to be an honour, and so, with my brother, Theodore, and sister, Josephine, left for Paris, where we were warmly welcomed by our cousins, Major and Madame Stuart Booth.

It was in the large Salvation Army Hostel for Women — le Palais de la Femme — that the meeting of commemoration was held. During this warm and friendly occasion, I was happy to give a brief message in French, and to sing one of the Maréchale's hymns, 'Vive Jésus des pécheurs l'espérence'. My brother read a passage from the New Testament. What a bond is ours as Christians. It transcends all time, change and circumstances, uniting us for ever in Christ.

Nevertheless, crises do happen, which can sever even the closest ties. Time and again, mighty movements of God have been assailed by the subtle tactics of the enemy.

At the end of the nineteenth century, General William Booth sent the Maréchale to Holland. She was then in her forties, and the last three of her ten children were born in Amsterdam. Her time there was by no means easy. She found it extremely difficult to master the language. However hard she tried, she never achieved the fluency in Dutch, vital to the personal work so dear to her heart.

She told the General that she was willing to go wherever French and English were spoken. But the discipline of the Army was such that the General expected the same obedience from his children as from his officers. The issues involved in this disagreement were many and complex. No one will ever know the cost on both sides.

I was privileged to have an inkling of my Mother's side of it, one day in the garden at the Haven. It was 1943. She was then eighty-three, and was tearing up some of the General's letters, written during the crisis. She was weeping. On realising my presence, she said softly, "I should never have left my Father."

There are moments in life, when we are given a glimpse of something deeply sacred. And if God prompts us to share that moment, hitherto hidden, however long and for whatever reason, we can be assured that it is for the blessing of others. The Maréchale's words, while betraying her pain, were much more a confession of her undying love for her Father.

Chapter 19

Stand up and Bless the Lord

"They loved not their lives to the death.
Christ only — their soul's vital breath,
O Lord, might I this lesson learn
To finish this course with joy,
With joy!"[1]

God does not allow our mistakes to frustrate His purposes. He has a way of using them for good.

Nehemiah's building of the wall of Jerusalem was team-work. Undaunted by the apathy of the Jews, the intimidation of the enemy, he pressed on without pause to a complete victory.

Victory with God

Nehemiah could be said to have reached the peak of his career, as cup-bearer to the king of Shushan, capital of the Persian court. But he was in exile. One day a messenger arrived from Jerusalem with devastating news,

"Those who survived the exile and are back in the province are in great trouble and disgrace. The wall of Jerusalem is broken down and its gates have been burned with fire." (Nehemiah 1:3 NIV)

1. To Sing Thy Praise, Book 1. Evelyn Booth-Clibborn

How did Nehemiah respond to that outburst?

He took it to heart

Success had not hardened him, nor had his own security made him indifferent to others. He was a godly man, and was extremely moved by the plight of his own people. Who could help in this impossible situation?

He took it to God

In His presence, Nehemiah immediately became aware of sin. He knew that with God the inner need was much greater than the outer need. He identified himself with the people,

"We have sinned . . ." (Nehemiah 1:6)

This is where we begin. There can be no victory with God until we acknowledge and confess our sin and utter unworthiness in His sight. This is the depth to which He brought me that early morning in New York.

Was Nehemiah then left without hope concerning his great problem?

He took it to the word

Oh, the living word. It shall not pass away.

"Remember the instructions you gave your servant Moses saying, 'if you are unfaithful, I will scatter you among the nations, but if you return to me and obey my commands, then even if your exiled people are at the farthest horizon, I will gather them from there and bring them to the place I have chosen as a dwelling for my Name'." (Nehemiah 1:8-10 NIV).

Nehemiah was repenting in the name of God's people, who were also repenting. He was claiming that God would gather them to the place He had chosen — Jerusalem — to restore its broken walls and burned-down gates, and to set His Name there.

Was not he applying the promise to the need, just as God enabled me to do that early morning when He gave me Isaiah 43 verse 19,

"I will make a way in the wilderness and rivers in the desert."? He cannot deny His word. This is victory with God.

Victory with man

Only at the very end of his intercession did Nehemiah mention his own personal dilemma.

"Give your servant success today by granting him favour in the presence of this man." (Nehemiah 1:11 NIV).

Nehemiah approaches the king

No outward sign did Nehemiah give of the inner distress, whatever the grief shown when he was alone. Any slight deviation from his high standard as the king's cup-bearer would have prejudiced the royal judgement with regard to a possible request. He was on duty at the king's table as usual, just as Samuel, after God's dramatic call during the night, was on duty early next morning, opening the doors of the Temple.

The world may not know about our prayer life, but it will discover very quickly if we neglect our responsibilities or falter in our conduct.

He had prayed that he might somehow influence the king, yet surprisingly, in view of the urgent need, he said nothing. Nothing at all. Why? Could it have been God's restraining hand? The Lord, perfect in wisdom, knew that it would be far more effective for the king to approach Nehemiah than for Nehemiah to approach the king. And that is just what happened.

When we commit our cause to God, we do not always have to speak or act right away. The delay may put us under considerable strain; but how much better it is to await God's time, God's way of acting.

The king approaches Nehemiah

"Why does your face look so sad when you are not ill?" (Nehemiah 2:2 NIV).

No. Nehemiah was not ill, and the king knew it.

"This," he said with a flash of insight, *"can be nothing but sadness of heart."*

Yes, and God wanted the king to see that sorrow, that godly sorrow.

In exciting the royal curiosity, Nehemiah was given an opportunity far surpassing anything he could have worked up for himself. Even though fear clutched at his heart because of this sudden opening, this breathless moment before taking the plunge (how would the king receive the news?), he nevertheless took that plunge. Was he not ready, on tip toe, as it were?

Are we ready when opportunity suddenly flings open a door? In spite of fear and trembling, will we seize the God-given moment then and there?

How many such openings are missed because we are not prepared?

There was no hesitation in Nehemiah's entry through that door, however small the opening. The very brevity of his reply shows how ready he was,

"Why should my face not look sad when the city where my fathers are buried lies in ruins, and its gates have been destroyed by fire?" (Nehemiah 2:3 NIV).

Even now Nehemiah did not ask for help. It was the king himself, with all the power and means of assisting him, who suggested that Nehemiah should make a request.

The promise continued to be applied to the need. Through the king, the gathering of God's people to His chosen place, Jerusalem, was to begin. How wonderfully God works when we await His own perfect timing.

"For what," said the king to Nehemiah, *"do you make request?"*

Up went a swift prayer to his God, and from that very moment all Nehemiah's needs were met.

So were mine at that time of my life when God brought me back from America to England, to His chosen place for me. In spite of much opposition to my going, God's provision for my journey came in a most remarkable way.

This is victory with man.

Victory with the work

God prepared Nehemiah for the task. He was in Jerusalem three days, rising at night to view the scene of the disaster,

"I had not told anyone what my God had put in my heart to do for Jerusalem." (Nehemiah 2:12 NIV).

O, if we could always begin there, *"consulting not with flesh and blood",* (Galatians 1:16) but with God alone concerning our problems.

God also prepared His people. Only after a time alone with God did Nehemiah speak to them all — Jews, priests, nobles and rulers — of the great work they faced, and call them to *"rise up and build".* So ready were they that their response was but the echo of his own words,

"Let us rise up and build." (Nehemiah 2:18)

Chapter three gives a detailed account of the steady building that followed.

Meanwhile, the enemy developed a plot to destroy Nehemiah and the people. Any visible work of God will inevitably draw enemy fire,

"When Sanballat and Tobiah and the Arabs and the Ammonites and the Ashdodites heard that the repairing of the walls of Jerusalem was going forward and that the breaches were beginning to be closed, they were very angry; and they all plotted together to come and fight against Jerusalem and to cause confusion in it." (Nehemiah 4:7-8).

But then came the information that their plot had become known to the people and that God had brought their counsel to nothing. Nehemiah, aware of this, gathered his people together and, *"we all returned to the wall, each to his work".* (Nehemiah 4:15) They could not get back quickly enough.

What an unspeakable asset it is when mind, heart and will are wholly given to the service of God, so that He and His people can work as one in the fulfilling of His great purposes. This is team-work in its truest sense.

It is not possible to succeed unequipped. Enemy activity inspired unity and efficiency; so now the builders stood in the breach, weapon (symbol of the sword of the Spirit — the Word of God) in one hand, and, with the other, the building continued.

The work went on. Then the enemy went for higher stakes. Their sights were set on Nehemiah alone. The attack came in the form of two temptations (Chapter Six). The first itself has three distinct aspects:

(i) Nehemiah was to come down from Jerusalem onto the plain, symbolising a descent from God's high purpose to the lower level of compromise;

(ii) Nehemiah was to meet for discussion on an impossible basis; for the enemy's counsel would be that of the ungodly, whilst his was that of the godly; and do we not read in Psalm 1 that the truly blessed man is the one that *"does not walk in the counsel of the ungodly"*. We are never told to argue with the enemy. We are asked only to shine, to witness and to teach;

(iii) Nehemiah was to forsake the task entrusted to him, and go into wholly unproved territory. This was enemy territory into which he would be going, and should not be entered without God's leading. That was the trouble with Peter in the servants' hall. He was in the wrong place, warming himself at the wrong fire. This temptation was brought to Nehemiah's attention no less than four times, but close touch with God had developed his powers of perception. Right from the start, he had seen the danger and resisted it. What a tiny word is 'no'; yet with God in it, how powerful! Nehemiah's eyes were never off the target.

"I am doing a great work," he told them. *"Why should the work stop while I leave it and come down to you?"* (Nehemiah 6:3 NIV).

Why indeed? The fact was that nothing was going to distract him from his task. Nothing.

Has something deflected you or me from the right path? Are we perhaps already in that valley, and finding it very hard to come up again? Suppose, having yielded to some temptation, we have fallen from His plan down to a lower level. My personal experience is that, provided we turn to God in true repentance, He Himself will bring us up, step by step, back into His plan for us. God only wants our willingness. He does the rest.

The second temptation was far more subtle and dangerous. It was rumoured, said Sanballat's servant, that Nehemiah was planning a rebellion, hence the building of the wall; that he himself was to be king, his prophets already claiming him as such. Again we see Nehemiah's God-given perception.

"Nothing like what you are saying is happening; you are just making it up out of your head." (Nehemiah 6:8 NIV).

Another proposal, made through a man hired by the enemy, was that they should meet together in the Temple, *"because men are coming to kill you — by night they are coming to kill you."* (Nehemiah 6:10 NIV).

Hurry, Nehemiah, hurry! But Nehemiah did not hurry. Viewing the wall, he had asked, *"Should such a work stop?"* Viewing himself, he could ask, *"Should such a men as I (God's man) flee?"* No, he would not use the house of God to save his own skin. It was unthinkable. *"I will not go in."* (Nehemiah 6:11).

This, the enemy's final attempt to stop the work, was but a dark back-drop to the immediate, shining declaration,

"So the wall was finished." (Nehemiah 6:15).

There will always be discomfiture among His opposers, when a work is so obviously of God.

"When all our enemies heard about this, all the surrounding nations were afraid and lost their self-confidence, because they realised that this work had been done with the help of our God." (Nehemiah 6:16 NIV).

That work had proceeded through victory with God, when Nehemiah claimed His promise to His people; victory with man, when the king was used to initiate the start of the work; and victory with the work itself, when God, through Nehemiah and the people, completed the wall.

This was irrefutable proof of all the patient, persistent work that had gone into it; of every single stone put into place; of each small breach filled in; of the daily, steady, unceasing labour, punctuated throughout with Nehemiah's brief, but powerful, prayers. God applied the promise to the need.

Ponder those prayers again. See how related to the task they were. Nehemiah's aim was to please God, and all his energies were directed to this end. Such perception, such persistence, such performance. Fifty-two days. That is all it took to complete the wall.

I have taken this subject many times. Is it because there is something so definite about

Nehemiah, a quality I esteem greatly? For so long I had drifted, unsure of my way. My upbringing had been one of strict routine. Perhaps it was reaction to this that made me so affected by the lighter emotional touches, whether in the spiritual atmosphere of Keswick, or in the light-heartedness of America.

I was never positive until I made a complete surrender to God of mind, heart and will. Then I knew where I was going. Whatever the temptations and trials, faults and failings, I have never taken back my will.

As opportunities for service came, I took them from the Lord. Whenever I prayed beforehand, I affirmed the victory, and would accept the task on that basis. I have never refused invitations, and God has always given me His power and fulfilled His word.

This is victory with the work.

Chapter 20

JUBILEE

"Strangers in the land, Lord,
Pilgrims bound for Home;
Tempted, tried and pressed, Lord,
Yet no more we roam;
For our goal is Jesus
That His will be done,
Children of the light, dear Master,
We are going on."[1]

In the spring of 1987, my life took a dramatic, though not unexpected, turn. Spring always inspires movement, and I have always been drawn towards the light, towards the morning of the day. By the end of June, I had moved from Slavanka to Seacliff Court.

I had said I could never move without God's 'green light'. When it came, the whole process was swift, uncomplicated and out of my hands. There was no strain.

My arthritis, coupled with a fall, necessitated the move, and some curtailment of activities. But the ministry to which God called me, whether by prayer, letter, interview or meeting, continues. His word to me then and now — as indeed to us all — is FORWARD! *"There remains yet very much to be possessed."* (Joshua 13:1)

1. To Sing Thy Praise, Book 2. Evelyn Booth-Clibborn.

Christmas 1988 Seacliff Court
23 Boscombe Cliff Road
Bournemouth
BH5 1JP

Dear Friend,

It is now well over a year since I arrived here at the end of June 1987, and I have been happily settling down in my new home.

The Lord has been so good in allowing me to carry on His work where I can have the care now become so essential.

Through the kindness of the management and the help of our prayer group, I was able to have a party here on Saturday, 30th. April, to mark my 90th birthday (27th. April).

Although the gathering could only be of a restricted number, it was wonderful. Friends God had blessed through the years gathered here from all parts of the country.

What was so apparent, right from the start, was the warmth and the pure joy experienced by all who were present. The household felt it too, and the door of the lounge being open, residents of Seacliff Court could hear whatever was said or sung in the hall.

A very good piano had been hired by some kind friends, and I was grateful to be able to play, not having touched the instrument for over twelve months. My niece, Joy, who has a good voice, led the singing of one or two of my songs.

Afterwards, we all, guests and residents, met in the dining-room to enjoy the excellent birthday tea, prepared by the staff, during which a note was handed to me, saying that your gifts for a telephone in my room came to the amazing total of well over £1,000! What a joy it is to have that convenience, and to be able to keep in touch. Thank you all so much.

My deepest desire for this special occasion was that we might together thank and praise the Lord to whom we owe so much.

While friends spoke again and again of the joy and freedom they felt on that day, comments perhaps even more significant could be summed up in the words of one who was present, "There was a deep sense of God's presence, and the whole afternoon resounded to His glory". This was God's wonderful answer to my prayer.

Perhaps the most striking moment of all for me personally was when I was reading from Deuteronomy, chapter 8, verse 2, to a group standing around me,

"And thou shalt remember all the way the Lord thy God has led thee these forty years."

Here I stopped, asking myself softly, "Was it forty years that He had led me?" "No," came the sudden surprise, "it was *fifty* years. Was it not in 1938 that I gave my life to God?"

There, standing among my friends, I realised for the first time that I was also marking the jubilee of my dedicated life — **fifty years for Jesus** — the longest, most spiritually fruitful part of my ninety years.

This gave the celebration a yet deeper cause for praise and thanksgiving to God, even for the forty years of spiritual wilderness which had led to that dedication, and since then, to the continual proving of God-given victory through our Lord Jesus Christ (1 Corinthians 15, verse 57).

May God bless you richly.

Yours ever faithfully in Christ,

Evelyn Booth-Clibborn.